JOE SCHMOE to the RESCUE!
Solving America's Problems

ROD STERLING

Copyright © 2014 Rod Sterling.

All rights reserved. No part of this book may be reproduced, stored, or transmitted by any means—whether auditory, graphic, mechanical, or electronic—without written permission of both publisher and author, except in the case of brief excerpts used in critical articles and reviews. Unauthorized reproduction of any part of this work is illegal and is punishable by law.

ISBN: 978-1-4834-1547-5 (sc)
ISBN: 978-1-4834-1548-2 (e)

Because of the dynamic nature of the Internet, any web addresses or links contained in this book may have changed since publication and may no longer be valid. The views expressed in this work are solely those of the author and do not necessarily reflect the views of the publisher, and the publisher hereby disclaims any responsibility for them.

Any people depicted in stock imagery provided by Thinkstock are models, and such images are being used for illustrative purposes only.
Certain stock imagery © Thinkstock.

Lulu Publishing Services rev. date: 8/11/2014

DEDICATION

This little book is dedicated to you, the reader, who, by the very act of opening and reading this book, or other books that discuss what has gone wrong in America, is combating those dangerous and evil stepbrothers known as apathy and complacency.

INTRODUCTION

I'm Joe Schmoe. Nobody special. Some people call me Joe Blow, Joe Doakes, John Doe, John Q. Public or the Man on the Street. I'm a husband, father, grandfather, brother and uncle. I'm an American. I was born in America and raised in America. I'm a veteran. I'm a dime a dozen. Nobody special.

I don't have a college degree. In fact, I didn't even graduate from high school in the traditional manner. After 3 1/2 years in the military while serving overseas - when I turned 21 - my home state mailed me a diploma based on a GED test. I'm just an average guy who's been around for a while. Seventy-four years. I made my living for fifty years with common sense and not being lied to. Common sense has become a scarcity in recent times. Like a lot of things that used to be good, it is now often frowned upon because it requires independent thinking.

People often complain about governmental or societal problems but offer no practical solutions. This is a no-whining zone. Major problems are presented herein accompanied by practical solutions. While politics creeps in here and there, it is common sense and logic that form the answers. You may think some solutions liberal and others conservative. Consideration was not given to either camp.

In seventy-four years, you figure some stuff out if you've kept your eyes and ears open. I don't mean to say that wisdom always accompanies age. There's no guarantee because a lot of people stopped thinking long before they got old, if they ever started. By the way, you'll notice there's not a lot of talk about wisdom anymore -- still more opposition to independent thinking.

I see people on television giving political opinion every day who would need flashlights to locate their own rear ends. Each of them has a vote that carries the same weight as mine. But each of them has a much bigger voice because somebody has put them on TV. This book is my effort to amplify my voice and that of the millions who agree with me.

I have written e-mails and letters to the local editorial page about some of these ideas in the past and opponents say "Did you research this?" That's just another way to say "You couldn't possibly come up with a solution. You must leave that to smarter people." The ideas expressed in this book are my opinions. I don't have to research my own opinions. Still others, who are inclined to agree, have said "But this would never get through congress." A sure way to keep it from getting through congress is to take that position. Congress, but for a very few exceptions, consist of people whose only real objective is to get re-elected. When 51% of the people want something, it will go through Congress.

When something is reduced to writing, it ought to clarify the issue, not obscure it. My mission is to present logical solutions to our nation's problems. No high-fallutin' theories and no color-coded graphs are used. These problems are offered in the order in which I wrote them. and not by any degree of importance.

I'm Joe Schmoe. Nobody special. There are millions like me.

CONTENTS

1. Campaign Finance Reform 1
2. Drugs 4
3. Global Warming.....Or Whatever They're Calling It Now 6
4. Health Plan 10
5. Keeping An Eye on CEO's 15
6. Racial Problems 17
7. Mass Murderers 22
8. Federal Debt 25
9. Single Issue Voters 30
10. Prison Reform 32
11. Public Sector Unions 34
12. The United Nations 38
13. Compromise 39
14. Length of Bills 41
15. The Government's Approach to Failed Experiments 42
16. National Defense 43
17. The Media and Its Dereliction of Duty 45
18. Counterfeit Logic and Don't Let the Lingo Fool You 53
19. The Minimum Wage 57
20. Red States/Blue States 59
21. Hollywood Liberals 61
22. Middle Class Liberals 65
23. Political Correctness and Taking/Giving Offense 69
24. Photo I.D. to Vote? 73
25. Taking the Fifth 77
26. The Biggest Problem of Them All: US 78

ONE

CAMPAIGN FINANCE REFORM

One of the truest and saddest things I ever heard from the lips of a congressman came from a former Philadelphia longshoreman, Michael Joseph "Ozzie" Myers. He was unknowingly addressing an undercover FBI agent dressed as a sheik in 1979.

"I'm gonna tell you somethin' real simple and short. Money talks in business and bullshit walks. And it works the same way down in Washington." Ozzie Myers became the first person expelled from congress since 1861.

Money is everything in political campaigns. The result is that while we all have a vote, we have almost nothing to say about who the two or three people are as candidates for any particular office. We often vote for the one we dislike least. The deepest pockets fill the airwaves by mud-slinging his opponent. Dirty politics works because if you hear a lie often enough, sooner or later you'll believe it.

Our current system wasn't designed for lobbyists but it's a perfect fit. We need campaign finance reform if only to take away the power of the lobbyists.

This is Joe Schmoes plan:

It shall be illegal to make any political contributions to any candidate for public office whether local, state or federal. It shall also be illegal for any candidate to receive any contributions.

Every taxpayer will be assessed $25.00 each year with his income tax return to fund all political campaigns. The money would be apportioned to go to local, state or federal elections proportionately. E.G. A senatorial candidate in Alaska would not have to reach as many people as his counterpart in Ohio and therefore would not receive as much money.

The only permitted political contributions would be to fund the gathering of petition signatures needed to qualify for a ballot position.

After the primary is over any surplus would be required to be turned over to the general fund. Not one penny could ever find its way into a candidate's pocket. No other contributions, whether in kind, personal, or corporate. could be made or received. Foreign donations, personal, corporate, or national, shall be prohibited even in the petition phase.

Any individual who violates this law, whether a donor, a recipient, or any person conspiring to subvert the intentions of this law, shall spend the next five years in a federal detention camp.

An opponent of this idea said: "But there are people who can't afford $25.00." This person clearly has no idea what is happening. Consider the role of a lobbyist. He is engaged to represent the interest of a particular business or industry. His weapon is holding the purse strings on moneys earmarked for political campaigns.

When a business or industry contributes money to a given candidate's campaign, it is because the business or industry has expectations of selling more of their product or service if that individual gets elected. That contribution becomes a cost of doing business and is reflected in the price of that product or service to the consumer. Often, that occurs at three levels: the manufacturer, the wholesaler and the retailer. The result is that a product could easily cost fifteen or twenty percent higher than what it could sell for with no political contribution factored in. The lobbyists are not exclusively in Washington, but operate in every state capitol as well.

And that happens with virtually all products or services: clothing, automobiles, fuel, furniture, food, insurance, interest rates. Everything.

How much extra does the average guy pay because of this system of political contributions? Impossible to say, but it would likely be at least a tenth of all you spend on goods and services: thousands of dollars.

So what it boils down to is not only are you paying for those television commercials for candidates, but you are supporting a system which minimizes your voice and maximizes the lobbyist's voice. You are paying to elect people that do not represent your interests, your political philosophy, your state or congressional district. So much for the guy who can't afford the $25.00.

This same process is in play at all levels of government. Consider the lawyer who wants to be named as city attorney. The county Republican or Democrat chairperson requests a political donation of $20,000 to help fund the campaigns of candidates to municipal and/or county office. It is understood that if the lawyer makes no contribution, he will not get the job. Again, the contribution becomes a cost of doing business and his rates are raised to recover such cost. And who pays that? The taxpayer. When you consider this system is applied to new police cars, coffee makers in the break room, or computers in the local library, it becomes apparent that much of your income exists to fund political campaigns.

Politicians have to spend a great deal of time not on serving the public that elected them, but in raising money for the next campaign. My plan would end that. Lobbyists would become an endangered species. Maybe a couple of Italian shoe companies would go under.

Applying this very simple system of everybody kicking in $25.00 a year would reduce costs all around and put the power back where it belongs: to the citizens.

When people hear about government corruption, they think about an official taking bribes or accepting expensive gifts in exchange for political favors. Corruption does include those things, of course, but most government corruption is perfectly legal. And it is perfectly legal because that is the way our elected officials want it to be.

Two

DRUGS

In 1933, after nearly fourteen years of prohibition of the manufacture or sale of alcoholic beverages, the American people wisely employed common sense and repealed the 18th Amendment to the Constitution, commonly known as the Volstead Act, or, officially, The National Prohibition Act.

The purpose of the Volstead Act was to rid society of the evils of drunkenness. It didn't accomplish that end but did foster an underground, tax-free industry, without quality control, that corrupted officials, fertilized crime waves, crowded our courts and filled up our prisons. People died or went blind drinking bad booze. And throughout the thirteen years, those who wanted to drink, drank.

Yet we persist in the prohibition of drugs, which has all the negative effects of alcohol prohibition and more. It is well past the time that drug use be legalized. And the word is legalized, not de-criminalized. Allow hard drugs to be sold by doctors' prescriptions. Sell marijuana like tobacco. Bureaucrats will try to cash in and tax it to the sky. I propose no opposition to taxing but suggest that not more than twenty-five percent of the ultimate retail price could go to taxes, divided up by local jurisdiction, state and federal government. The price, and therefore the tax, could only be raised by the retailer. For this plan to succeed, the price must be very substantially reduced to take the criminal element out of the equation. If the price goes higher and higher, drug dealers will re-surface and undercut legitimate prices.

Opponents will argue that drug use will increase. I think not. Firstly, no doctor would issue a prescription to anyone who was not already addicted. And criminal drug dealers would dry up because they would not have repeat business. Who would pay $40 or $50 for a daily fix when a prescription for the same thing would cost only a dollar or two?

It is, after all, the contraband element that keeps the price sky-high. With legalization, the prices would plummet. I have also been told by several former druggies that "making the *score*" was part of the thrill. If marijuana was for sale at the 7-11 for pocket change, the rebellious thrill is gone.

Consider the benefits. It is estimated that about thirty percent of the prison population, county, state or federal, is for drug related crimes. Add to that people who were convicted of robbery, burglary, prostitution or auto theft who committed the crime to fund a drug habit, and likely half the people in jail are there because of drug prohibition.

The cost to the taxpayers for police, prison guards, probation officers, social workers, Federal Drug Enforcement Agency, and other personnel would be substantially reduced.* Court calendars would be eased. Gang warfare is largely turf wars for drug sales. Illegal aliens often act as couriers for foreign grown or manufactured drugs. Take the money out of it and the border problems are diminished.

It's been said that insanity is doing the same thing over and over and expecting different results. Prohibition on drugs has been in place for over one hundred years. It gets worse every year and the "war on drugs" is costing us many billions of dollars annually.

Let's call for a cease fire.

* For those who oppose this because of fewer government jobs, it should be recognized that government does not exist to provide employment. The fact that it does provide employment to many -- far too many -- supports the argument to legalize drugs. Public employees will still exist, but only the ones we need. If crime is reduced by fifty percent, we certainly will not need the same strength of employees to deal with it.

Three

GLOBAL WARMING.....Or Whatever They're Calling It Now

I took my last science class - high school biology, where a frog is dissected - about the time Elvis Presley was making his debut on the Ed Sullivan Show. So I know next to nothing about science.

I finally accepted the "expert testimony" that the earth was in a warming cycle. I probably would have come to that opinion sooner but the WARMERS kept talking about a hole in the ozone layer the size of Arkansas that was the result of human beings burning stuff. They said the hole was over Antarctica. Two things gave rise to me not trusting them. If the hole was the result of industry and automobile emissions, why was it over the South Pole where there are no industries or automobiles? Why not over Pittsburgh? The second thing I noticed is that it was always Arkansas they compared it to, never North Carolina, New York or Alabama, each of which is virtually the same size as Arkansas.

I very definitely had the impression that the WARMERS got together and conspired with one another:

"Tell the idiots out there that we found this hole in the ozone layer that is real big."

"How big? Big like an elephant or big like Texas?"

"Something in between. Say it's as big as.....Arkansas."

"Arkansas is the same size as Alabama, or North Carolina, or New York. Why don't we say New York?"

"Don't confuse the issue. They know about New York. Most of them don't even know where Arkansas is. It'll scare the beejesus out of them. We're going with Arkansas. Pass it on." Because it was always Arkansas, it was obvious there was some organized movement and I sensed being the target of manipulation. Nevertheless, by 2005, I was willing to accept Earth was in a warming cycle. Despite my limited formal education, I knew the earth had gone through other cycles long before Henry Ford came along, the ice age, etc. I presumed the earth had a constantly changing climate pattern. By 2005, the Arkansas thing was no longer being discussed. Apparently, that was because it came out that the Arkansas hole had been there the first time they looked for it, and therefore was probably always there. In fact, maybe life on Earth owes its very existence to it being there to let the heat out.

So I was waiting for some evidence that humankind was the cause of the warming. Instead, Al Gore came up with the battle cry of "THE DEBATE IS OVER!"

"It's over?" I said. "Was I out taking a piss when somebody presented proof that the change is caused by man? What do you mean, it's over?"

Next I heard a spokesman for the WARMERS talking about how many scientists agreed we were in a world-wide warming cycle. The spokesperson was not a scientist, of course, but a political pundit.

"The consensus of the scientific community is that we're in a man-made warming cycle." Consensus? Isn't that a political word? It sure isn't a scientific word. What's the consensus on H2O being water? Isn't it 100%? So are the scientists voting now instead of getting proof through experiments? "All in favor of global warming, say aye. Looks like the ayes have it." I began to distrust the scientists who I reasoned were selling out for grant money. Some scientists have surfaced saying global warming support is a prerequisite to receiving grant money. I noticed that people who are always badmouthing the USA were more often WARMERS than not. What was supposed to have been pure science, is, in fact, pure politics.

They were cherry-picking information and presenting it falsely. Take the mama polar bear picture. The WARMERS disseminated a photograph of a mama polar bear with two cubs on an ice floe the size of a pickup truck. All that can be seen in the picture, beside the bears and the ice floe is endless ocean. The implication was these poor bears have been left with nothing but a tiny ice floe to keep them out of the frigid sea. After this photo got around for a year or so, the photographer surfaced. He said that it was not his intention to convey that message when he snapped the shot. "Out of the frame of the picture, not twenty yards away, was an ice mass the size of New England. The bears swam out and were playing."

Then came the destruction of the scientific data for as long as records have been kept on weather. This took place in the Climate Research Unit at the University of East Anglia, in Norwich, England. There are four possibilities of what those records could have indicated:

1. That mankind was responsible for global warming.
2. That nothing conclusive could be ascertained from the records.
3. That global warming was NOT under way.
4. That global warming was a fact but the records tended to indicate that similar patterns existed before the industrial revolution, and therefore not brought about by mankind.

I submit that if it was either number one or number two, those records would still be intact. The scientists at that institution concluded the records indicated no significant temperature increase world wide as a result of mankind and that didn't suit the political agenda of those funding them. So the records were destroyed. Their flimsy excuse was they had to make room for current records. Isn't that what computers are for? The nicest thing I can say about the people responsible is they are book burners.

I, therefore, have it on good authority -- and so do you -- that either global warming does not exist or if it does exist mankind is not responsible for it. The scientists themselves revealed their true belief when they destroyed the records. Common sense and logic tell you there could be no other reason to destroy the records.

One woman told me that it was naive to deny global warming. I believe it is incredibly naive to ignore the destruction of the records.

Everyone should ask themselves what reason could there be for such destruction of the records. Certainly it was not to make space for current records. Kiss me before you lie to me.

In George Orwell's classic 1948 book, "1984," the political leaders set off explosives five miles outside of London to support their false claim that England was under attack by an enemy. People were manipulated into believing their country was at war to explain the rationing, curfews etc.

Orwell was a visionary. Global Warming is the 21st Century equivalent of Big Brother.

Four

HEALTH PLAN

The first thing to recognize about health care is that it never has been free, never will be free and never should be free. It is something of value and it must be paid for. The Affordable Care Act (ACA) reminds me of an old Aesop's Fable. It's the one about the dog with the bone is his mouth crossing a stream on a footbridge. Halfway out on the bridge, he looks over the side and see his own reflection in the still water. He perceives the reflection to be some other dog who also has a bone. He growls in the hope that the other dog will be scared away and drop the bone in his haste. Of course, when he growls, he loosens his grip on his own bone, and it drops into the deep water. The ACA, often referred to as ObamaCare, purported to provide free or nearly free health care for the poorest Americans with the result that many formerly insured people have been left high and dry, and many others are paying much more, and the original uninsured are still uninsured. Obama growled and lost his bone.

There were about thirty million people uninsured. Many of them were uninsured by choice. Usually these would be young, healthy, single people who opted to spend the money on something else, such as a jet ski. The people behind the ACA claimed to be concerned about those thirty million and a ludicrous bill containing a million words passed through first the Senate and then the House of Representatives. It is now in the process of collapsing under its own weight. Meanwhile, it has screwed up the pre-existing plans and has left the country in turmoil. And now the government's independent offices have indicated that it will cost many jobs and we will still have thirty million uninsured.

I could write a whole book criticizing the ACA, but this essay is about the solution. This is a common sense plan which when adopted will accomplish the following:

* Cover every single American and legal alien who enrolls.
* Reduce health care expense by at least 20%.
* Create a cost to the federal government of no more that thirty billion with at least half being recoverable.
* Increase new private sector jobs and save many existing jobs.
* Reduce expenses to the separate states of about $200 billion in total.
* Relieve the federal government of the fiscally impossible task of funding Medicare.
* Relieve our courts of many law suits.
* Render entry into all phases of the medical field more, not less, attractive to our youth.
* Put the management of medical treatment back into the hands of doctors and not insurance companies and federal bureaucrats.
* Remove the risk of financial devastation to individuals, medical practitioners and hospitals.
* Reduce, yes, reduce the cost of health care to the individual subscribers.

FIRST, bring about tort reform. Create a reasonable set of guidelines and limitations to put an end to excessive awards in litigation. Currently, an insurance company has no idea of the extent of the risk and cannot accurately calculate the premium. In self protection, the premium is figured on the high side with the result that medical practitioners often pay in the hundreds of thousands dollars annually to be covered when sued by a patient. The cost of the premium is passed along to all the doctor's patients.

Comment: Plaintiffs' attorneys often persuade juries to "punish" the offending medical practitioner or hospital with outlandishly excessive awards, without the jury understanding that such punishment is passed along in increased insurance premiums. It is a shortcoming of people in general to want to "stick it to the man," without realizing they are sticking it to themselves and others like them.

This plan would also tend to reduce tests ordered by physicians for almost no other reason than to protect themselves from their own patients.

SECOND, terminate health plans of every federal employee (except the military) including all 545 members of the legislative, judicial and executive branches. Terminate Medicare. Urge in every legal manner that the respective states follow suit with all state, county and municipal workers. Urge in every legal manner that all private employers no longer offer medical plans as a perquisite for employment, including union employees. One measure would be to disallow employee medical plans as a corporate write-off on tax returns. All employers, private and public, would be encouraged to increase salary levels to offset individual costs outlined in paragraph THIRD, below.

Comment: We must divorce ourselves from the notion that public employees are somehow superior to those in the private sector. Standard health care entitlement in public employment must end. It should be noted that many public employees are married to other public employees and carry double coverage needlessly since each spouse is covered under the spouse's plan. In some cases, employment is gained in public service after retirement from other public service and triple and even quadruple coverage exists at tax payer expense.

By separating health care from employment, the disincentive to create new hires is reduced substantially. Many employers took on the burden of paying for health care in lieu of salary increase at a time when health care was relatively cheap. Now the government has made it mandatory or financially penalizing to those who do not so provide.

This plan will help bring about a healthier ratio of public to private workers. Everyone cannot work for the government.

THIRD, every family unit will pay all medical costs up to 5% of their gross annual income in any given year. The "gross annual income" is literally all income including pensions, social security, tax-free bonds, all government subsistence. etc. "Family unit" is defined as just one person, or a traditional family of husband, wife, children, if any, or other handicapped or disabled adult dependents.

Individuals are to be encouraged to open MEDICAL SAVINGS ACCOUNTS. (Passed by congress in 2004). The MSA should have the maximum tax-free amount increased to 10% of gross income. Withdrawals from such account for non-medical reasons shall be subject to fines, back taxes and interest. Such account shall be set aside from bankruptcy proceedings.

The federal government shall issue a medical card or cards to all enrollees. Such card can be used to obtain treatment. If the hospital or doctor who provided treatment has not received payment from the individual within thirty days, an invoice is sent to the federal government who will make the payment within an additional thirty days. The federal government shall recover the expense with the income tax return of the person who incurred the charge, or forgiven, in full or part, for special hardship cases.

Elective or cosmetic surgery shall not be included as medical costs other than to correct deformity or disfigurement. Over the counter drugs shall not be included as medical costs.

Illegal aliens shall be denied other than emergency medical treatment.

Comment: young and healthy people could often build up substantial sums in the MSA's, even $50,000 to $100,000 before beginning a family or incurring rising medical expenses normally occurring in later life. Such sums could be drawn upon to pay the up front medical expense (the first 5%) and/or the premium for excess limits insurance discussed in paragraph FIFTH below.

It is estimated that the federal government would have an outlay of twenty to thirty billion, of which about two-thirds would be recovered through the IRS

FOURTH, the state of residence shall insure each family unit for medical expense between the 5% of gross income and the sum of $35,000. Each state will be under great pressure to enact such legislation because the alternative will be that most of their citizens will be uninsured. Enacting the legislation will mean that all state, county and municipal employees will no longer have medical plans with their employment.

Comment: It is estimated that the state will bear expenses in the range of $900 to $1,200 per state resident. Each state currently spends about $2,000 per resident on the medical plans of public employees, which expense the state would no longer be incurring.

FIFTH, each family unit shall carry an excess limits policy for medical expense that exceeds the $35,000 level and up to, say, $3 million. This type of policy is not expensive and would cost about $1,000 to $2,000 per annum depending on the size of the family. A number of insurance industry people have estimated the cost to be about $500 per person. The insurance carriers licensed to provide excess limits policies in any given state would be compelled to include those family units with pre-existing conditions or aged members at the same cost as to similarly sized families.

Comment: Under this plan, a person with only $25,000 in gross income would have a maximum exposure of $2,750. At $50,000; $4,000. At $75,000; $5,250. At $100,000 $6,500. At $200,000; $11,500 Those numbers include the up front 5% plus the excess limits premium.

On pre-existing conditions, it is clear that every human being is vulnerable to developing a condition, and the following year that condition becomes a pre-existing condition.

Therefore, all family units contributing to the insurance pool shall pay a premium which reflects that some family members will develop a condition. Under the old system, such a person may be excluded from coverage.

The concept of insurance is for each member of a pool of insured, to contribute a small sum to create a large fund protecting all the insured members against a travesty, in such event. This is a sound system. Let's get back to it.

It is common sense for the person receiving treatment to pay the first 5%. Auto insurance, which works a lot better than health insurance, does not cover oil changes. Any attempt to try to do so results in a fiasco such as the ACA, and the bone drops out of your mouth and into the river.

It should be noted that this particular essay contains about 1,600 words or 16/100 of one percent of Obamacare. And unlike Obamacare, this plan would actually work.

Five

KEEPING AN EYE ON CEO'S

This is more of a corporate problem than a government problem, although government entities such as Fannie Mae and Veterans Affairs caught the disease as well. Nothing is more disheartening to the public that some chief executive received a bonus of sixty million dollars. And often that occurs in a company that is not doing well.

This is America, and being America, no maximum earnings mandate can be issued by government. Pro ball players often receive huge amounts as well. Somehow, that goes down better with the guy on the street. And that is how it has to be.

There is nothing, however, in the law that prohibits the publication of salaries, bonuses and other perquisites of top executives in publicly owned companies. Envision private enterprise creating a website listing such salaries and bonuses, but translating it for the general public. Sunshine is the best antiseptic.

There might be an "employee index." The number of 550 would mean that the executive received 550 times the average salary paid in that corporation. Another index might show the relationship of the compensation to the corporate profit or loss. It might further stipulate what the distribution to stockholders would have been with lesser bonuses. Corporate annual reports sent to stockholders are notorious for complying with the law and delivering the facts but doing it in such a way to minimize objection. The facts as presented by this proposed website just might cause would be investors to pass up that corporation.

A prospective purchaser of insurance sees that a certain insurance company spends $110 million on executive bonuses. The website might show that premiums could be reduced by 12% if the bonuses were only $10 million. The potential customer looks elsewhere for coverage.

If I were young I would create that website. And America would be a better place for it.

Six

RACIAL PROBLEMS

What does the black community want? By "black community" I don't mean all black people. I mean Jesse Jackson, Al Sharpton, Barack Obama, Eric Holder, Maya Angelou, Jeremiah Wright, Julian Bond, Van Jones and a host of other black leaders or activists.

The last American slave holder died about the time I was born in 1940. The last American born into slavery died about the time I reached my majority in 1961. However, it must be noted that during the first one hundred years following reconstruction (1865-1965) about five thousand blacks were lynched by racist vigilantes. That's about one a week. But that's been over for fifty years now.

For the last forty years, blacks have had full governmental equality, which is all any of us has, and, essentially, all there is to get.

What follows are generalizations on American black people. No one needs to point out exceptions. Of course, there are exceptions. Let's be honest in discussing the American black.

He is warm and humorous. He is neither lazy nor stupid. He often makes a great soldier, athlete or entertainer.

Occasionally reports surface indicating his IQ is several points lower than that of Europeans and their descendants, which are several points lower than Asians and Sephardic Jews. Critics of these reports have said that the IQ tests were created by European descendants and if they had been created by African descendants, the story might be different. The author is inclined to agree, but anyway, we're only talking about a couple of points. IQ is not nothing, but it sure is not everything. Ronald

Reagan's IQ was, in the author's estimation, probably twenty points below Jimmy Carter's, but who did the job and who didn't?

There is racism. There's good racism and bad racism. Bad racism is the lynch mobs discussed above and those bastards who chained a black guy to a pickup truck some ten or fifteen years ago. Good racism involves the liberal progressive who look upon the black people as inferior and wants the government to help them out. I suspect that the last fifty years of good racism has done as much damage to the American blacks as the hundred years of bad racism.

The author once made a tongue-in-cheek proposal to a news group that was made up almost entirely of liberals. "Let's support a federal measure to help Jewish people better understand the value of education and offer to fund it for them." They stared at me as if I were crazy.

"They know all about that. Why would we do that?"

"We do it for the blacks. In your refusal to do it for the Jews, aren't you saying they're superior to the blacks and conversely that the blacks are inferior to Jews?"

As a further example of the hypocrisy, take a look at the issue of using the dreaded "N" word. Blacks commonly use it and the liberals are okay with that. But if a white person uses it, he's finished. He's out of a job or worse. Why do white liberals condone blacks using the "N" word? Answer: Because they believe the blacks cannot be held to the same standard as the whites. If a raccoon turns over your garbage can, you put a cinder block on top of it. But if your neighbor's teen-aged kid does it, you call the cops. You don't hold the raccoon to the same standard as the teen-aged human. The liberals killing the blacks with kindness stems from the mistaken idea that the blacks are somehow inferior.

The most overt example of American racism in many years occurred in the 2012 presidential election. We will ignore that 95% of the blacks voted for Obama in 2008 because that was the first time a black man had a shot at the oval office. But his first term was a failed presidency. Obama demonstrated that he had neither the experience nor the integrity for the job. Nevertheless, 93% of them voted for him again. That means that about half of them - at a minimum - voted racially. But even Fox News didn't report that. Why not?

There is a a cable talk show in the morning with a couple of hosts and usually two or three guests and they talk over current events. About five years ago, a woman who is one of the hosts had mentioned off camera that she had been mugged that day by a black man when she left her apartment building in New York for a morning jog. She had no purse but had Starbuck's money in her pocket, which he took, but did not harm her. During the show, one of the guests commented on it and asked her if she had notified the police. She looked at him horrified.

"Of course not! All I had was six dollars." She was sympathetic that the poor fellow risked committing a felony and netted only six bucks. Her position was exactly, not similar, but *exactly*, as if she'd been asked if she wanted an Irish Setter locked up in a cage for the next three years for peeing on her leg.

The result is that treating the blacks as inferior people and giving them handouts for three generations has prepared many of them for nothing better. Killing with kindness is not the way to go. Do they have problems? They certainly do.

But no national voice is discussing their problem for fear of being accused of racism. A far too great a percentage of their young men and women have no grasp on delayed gratification and lapse into crime, drugs and prostitution at early ages. A black adolescent that tries to study and stay in school is often ridiculed as trying to be white. The ability for a teen to ignore peer pressure is reinforced by a nuclear family: a strong mother *and* father. It is in that setting that the value of setting a goal is taught.

The American black achieved full governmental equality forty years ago and it is high time he took greater responsibility for his own life. *(Admittedly, many blacks have done so, and also admittedly, there are many whites on welfare and food stamps, but with a much lower percentage.)*

There are a bunch of race hustlers: Jeremiah Wright, Jesse Jackson, Al Sharp ton, Henry Louis Gates (of Obama's beer summit fame). They continue to blame the white man for failing to provide still more assistance. These people have made careers of expostulating about the downtrodden black man and cannot let go. The fear being anachronistic. When a Jeremiah Wright stands at his pulpit and condemns white

America, he is saying: "Your problems are not your fault. It is the evil white man who is to blame. You don't have to change - HE DOES!"

The votes had hardly been counted giving Obama the 2008 election when Jackson and Sharpton were out there saying: "Racism is not over!" Jackson was so unnerved by the election of a black man to the nation's highest office (albeit, not Jesse Jackson), so scared that his movement was now anachronistic, that he lashed out and said he wanted to "cut Obama's nuts off." He carelessly said this in front of an open mike.

It is time that everyday responsible black people recognize that the best way to make an enemy is to treat someone like an enemy. Turn off the Jacksons, Sharptons, Wrights, Holders, and yes, Obamas. They are not in your corner. They're out for themselves.

A responsible black minister who cares about his flock - and they exist - says "You've got equality. Now let's see you use it. Stay in school. Stay out of jail. Stay with the women you've impregnated. Stay with the children you've sired. Stay sober. Stay off drugs. Stay employed."

If the real problem of the black people cannot be addressed, then it cannot be corrected. Everyone is terrified of being labeled racist. The author once complained about Barack Obama violating the U.S. Constitution, which he has done many times. A liberal said that was a racist comment.

The author's reply was: "Racism is legal, violating the constitution is not." The libs attack the messenger when they cannot argue the issue. By that logic, when I opposed John F. Kennedy allowing government workers to unionize, I was anti-Irish-Catholic, even though I am an Irish-Catholic.

The day after Barack Obama was elected in 2008, the author sat in front of the local supermarket at a cafe table with a container of coffee and a long puss. Three young black women got out of a car, giddy with delight over the election. As they passed by, one stopped and said: "Sir, you put a smile on your face, and you do it right now! And don't you worry none because everything is going to be alright."

The author laughed out loud and that broke the depression. And only then came the thought: *What is the up side of this election? There's always an upside. Of course! This is the end of this race problem we have been laboring under!"* But it was not the end of the race problem and it was not the end because all the blacks mentioned above - including Barack Obama - plus plenty of others both white and black, didn't want the race problems to be over because it did not suit their political agenda.

Solution: Support the decent working black people. Discuss the real issues with black youth. Provide the support they need to resist peer group pressure to take drugs or become part of a street gang. Remove incentives for government subsidy that favor a fatherless household. Begin to wean them off the concept that government will provide for them their entire lives. Instill in them the desire to live with dignity. Mainly, the problems have to be addressed publicly. If they can't be discussed without somebody's career being over, then they can't be corrected. The liberal movement does not want the problems corrected because they need a permanent underclass to continue their existence.

And if anyone feels the need to appoint a federal official to oversee this, make it Bill Cosby. He is one of the very few black people who have stepped up to the plate and told the truth.

Seven

MASS MURDERERS

We know who the people are that will tote an automatic rifle into a theater or school or supermarket and shoot the joint up. Collectively, we know who they are. But it happens anyway with increasing frequency because the information is not shared. At the rate of recent shootings or bombings, it would be reasonable to make preparations that over the next ten years, there may well be as many as fifty or sixty such incidents.. How do we protect ourselves and our children from murderous attacks?

There are plenty of people around saying "get rid of the guns." And while you're at it, get rid of category five hurricanes and California forest fires. There are more than one hundred million gun owners in America. Be logical.

Here is a workable alternative that would diminish these atrocities substantially. It won't eliminate them, unfortunately.

Human beings, at least some human beings, are highly perceptive. One of the most stupid things to come out of government in the last twenty years was this ban on what they call profiling. What does that mean? It means, we, the government, don't trust you, the policeman on the street, to use your natural intelligence, your clinical experience, your training or your instincts to protect yourselves and those you serve. Treat an old lady with a walker precisely the way you treat three young men in a car at 3:00 A.M.

There are people who give off an alarm. Danger! Danger! Danger! Lots of people sense it and try to avoid the person. There is nobody to explain this to.

Consider these shooters are usually young, teen-aged or early twenties. Many of them are reclusive but don't live in a vacuum. Lots of people crossed their paths School mates, teachers, neighbors, co-workers, relatives, or merchants in their communities. These people have seen their reactions to everyday situations, have seen them setting fire to kittens or acting abnormally. And yes, they have seen their eyes.

Create a body within the FBI or Homeland Security of, say, one hundred people trained in human behaviorism. Promote an 800 telephone number and E-mail address to give people a place to go when they sense a person is dangerous and potentially harmful.

These would not be accusations, but suspicions. The trained behaviorist would not only take the information down on the subject of the call but would analyze the caller. Malicious or baseless calls could, in most instances, be identified. The clinical experience of the staff would, far more often than not, know which calls to act upon, and which ones not to pursue.

The caller could not be anonymous to the behaviorist because identifying the caller, or the caller's willingness to identify himself, would be a major element in determining the validity of the call. But that name would never go any further. The caller would never have to fear reprisals, or being labeled as being prejudiced or racist. *Think about how many army officers at Fort Hood must have known that crazy doctor was a danger but were unwilling to risk their careers in fingering him.*

When the behaviorist concludes the subject's profile warranted keeping an eye on him, he would notify local law enforcement. The subject has not done anything as yet that would cause the police to arrest him, but would rather put them on alert.

Suppose the chief of police in Newtown, Connecticut had received four or five such reports on Adam Lanza over the span of a couple of years. Might he have learned that the boy's mother was, in fact, a straw buyer for automatic weapons? And then might he have had a confidential talk with her? Might he have disseminated photos and alerted his officers to keep a watchful eye on that youth when they observed him? Would that have averted the tragedy? Who can say? But I will tell you that if I was a neighbor of that kid, I would have made the call. And if I was the chief of police and got those reports, I sure wouldn't have ignored them. I think I would contact the subject just to take a good look at him myself. Oops Profiling!

This bank of suspected persons might grow to ten thousand, or even fifty thousand. And from that group there are fifty or sixty who may commit a mass murder over the next ten years.

This much is clear. It is a whole lot easier to deal with even fifty thousand possible mass shooters than with one hundred million gun owners.

These shooters have something in common; they are capable of committing evil irrational crimes. Instead of dealing with that commonality, which is possessed by a relatively small group, the anti-gun people go to another commonality, being gun owners, which is probably one out of every three people in the country. The mathematical solution of the anti-gun people is so illogical as to conclude their viewpoint is, in fact, a political one.

Many that oppose this measure are, almost certainly, those that lack the perceptiveness themselves and are disinclined to accept the fact that others are equipped with it. They always start talking about violating a person's rights. But the subject's rights are not being violated. If a policeman talks to a mother who is buying automatic weapons advising her to keep them locked up and out of her son's hands, has he violated the son's right?

I am a supporter of the Constitution of the United States and that includes the second amendment. But if I were running the National Rifle Association, I would have stipulated years ago that private citizens have no reason to own a magazine holding in excess of fifteen rounds.

But turning in one's guns? Only a law abiding person would do that. And then where would we be? The opponents to private ownership of guns never consider that the criminal element is well aware that lots of people are armed and act accordingly. As the bumper sticker says, "If guns are outlawed, only outlaws will have guns."

Eight

FEDERAL DEBT

When my daughter was eleven years old, she left her bedroom where she was doing homework and put a question to me: "If the government needs more money, why don't they just print it?" I answered her with a pocket sized checkbook, containing ten blank checks.

"Assume there is one thousand dollars in the account. If I used the ten checks each made out for the same amount, what would the amount be to spend all the money in the account?"

"$100 each," she answered.

"Right. But now if I instead got a brand new book of checks - there are 25 checks in a new book - what would be the amount then?"

"$40." she answered.

"So, the value of each check is diminished by printing more checks." She nodded understanding and went back to her homework.

At the age of eleven, she then knew more about the economy than well over half the voters in America, who somehow do not understand -- or mindlessly choose to ignore -- that ten dollars cannot be spent for every six dollars in income. The federal debt is approximately 17.5 trillion dollars as this is written. The cost, between interest payments incurred by borrowing and printing new money now approaches fifty percent of the gross federal revenues.

Before efforts can be made to reduce such a gargantuan debt, first spending in excess of income has to stop. At an earlier time, the federal government was limited to providing armed forces for defense, the minting of money and a postal system. That was basically it. We have to work backwards eliminating those things that the feds never should have gotten involved in.

In the blizzard of zeros that accompany federal spending, it becomes unfathomable to all, and most people simply adopt a complacent attitude that somehow it will work out. To attack the complacency, there was a simple example going around a couple of years ago:

    Federal Spending .... $ Three Point Eight Trillion
    Federal Gross Revenues ..... $ Two Point Two Trillion
    Federal Debt .... $ Sixteen Trillion
    Federal Budget Cut .... $ Thirty Eight Billion

For the sake of comprehension, this was reduced to the annual Jones Family budget with eight zeros being removed from each number:

    Yearly expenditures $38,000
    Yearly Income 22,000
    Credit Card Debt 160,000
    Yearly Spending Reduction 380

There are many that will say this is too simple and the overall economy cannot be understood by people who are untrained. In other words, "Sit back and don't try to understand that which is beyond you. Drink your beer, watch TV and don't forget to vote the Democratic ticket. We went to Harvard (or Yale or Duke) and we know what's best."

Another argument against fiscal sanity is to throw down a challenge: "You talk about cutting expenses but you don't say how. What would you reduce?"

"I thought you'd never ask."

    *   Health Plan - By utilizing the health care plan contained in this book, an estimated $160 billion federal dollars would be saved. The Government Accounting Office estimates ObamaCare will cost 1.8 trillion over ten years. My health plan would cost an estimated 300 billion over ten years with at least half half being recoverable.

* Drug legalization
* Prison Reform
* Welfare Reform
* US Dept of Energy - Shut it down. It was created in 1971 to reduce our dependency on foreign oil. We were then importing 30% of oil consumed. It is now 70%. It is a failed experiment. End it.
* Environmental Protection Agency - Shut it down. It is a power mad entity that is anti-business and costs untold amounts in lost revenues and employment for our people. Each state has a similar agency. Why the bureaucratic overkill? Understand that anything that is anti-business is anti-job. Put an end to the EPA.
* US Dept of Education - Shut it down. Each state has its own department of education. Stop interfering.
* US Dept of Labor - Shut it down. Again, Let each state handle their own disputes. They might actually know what's going on within their own borders.
* Drug Enforcement Administration - Shut it down. It won't be needed when drugs are legalized.
* Foreign Aid - Set up standards for recipients of American Foreign Aid. First and always: Only to friends. At the first sign of a burning American flag, forget getting any future checks. You're done! If you want our people and their money - personal or corporate - then we will need an embassy. If you don't provide external security for our embassy, you're out of the club. Not another penny. We frown on your misbehavior to your own people who don't support your regime, but if you're going to do it anyway, we suggest the ones you should kill are the anti-Americans. They are the ones who will cost you money
* Membership in U.N. - Let's stop participating in still another failed experiment.
* Increase the population for each member of the House of Representatives to one million, with low populated states being guaranteed at least one representative, thereby reducing the

number of representatives and their huge staffs by about one-quarter. No gerrymandering, follow county lines.
* Adoption of the Campaign Finance Reform, mentioned earlier in this book, would, of itself, save hundreds of billions of dollars.
* Those federal bureaucracies who survived termination would be required to reduce their personnel by twenty percent. Those terminated would be proportional to their G.S. rank - 20% of GS 15's, 20% of GS 10s, etc. After two years, go back and reduce it again. States, counties, and municipalities would be under some pressure from their citizens to follow suit.
* Get rid of every elected or appointed person in Washington who thinks the deficit does not matter. Believe it or not, that's well over half of them. Any print or electronic media or any politician that refers to someone speaking out to reduce spending as an extremist is lying to you. Elected officials who urge spending reductions of only five or six percent have been so labeled. The extremists are the ones who would continue with the excessive spending. Get them out of office.

After we do this, then we take a look at whether we are balancing the budget and if not, then we cut some more.

A couple I have known since high school married a year after graduation. In their twenties they had six children. They became grandparents in their middle forties and for the next fifteen years posted no less than eighteen grandchildren. They now have seven great-grandchildren. Totaling all four generations equals thirty-three people and growing. Recently they had a group photo taken. They all wore purple tee shirts and khaki trousers. It looked like the annual barbecue of the Mormon Tabernacle Choir.

This generational exponential growth mimics the federal government over the last eighty years. Agencies beget departments, departments beget divisions, divisions beget groups or committees. A mandate should go out demanding that every single entity justify its existence to an independent committee (yes, I am suggesting another committee), which might be called a flying squad of efficiency experts. Any entity that cannot justify their existence, shut it down. In eight or ten years, we can probably get rid of at least half, maybe three-quarters of them.

Once the feds put something into place, it's forever, whether it works or not. One such example was that during WWII, wool was needed for military uniforms and farmers were subsidized as an incentive to raise sheep. That subsidy did not end with WWII. Around 1960, wool was no longer needed for the uniforms. It was replaced with synthetics, but the subsidies continued on into 1993, when it was concluded. By then they were in the fourth generation of sheep farmers who believed it was a rightful and necessary entitlement. Their lobbyists got the subsidy back a couple of years later.

The flying squad investigating these various entities, will produce or be replaced. Their findings are reported to congress to be acted upon. Congressmen whose constituents will be affected -- adversely or positively -- would be required to recuse themselves. A congressman from Idaho would not be permitted to vote on the elimination of a federal potato department.

This approach can be handled in one of two ways: one to reduce unnecessary bureaucracy and two, to give the appearance of doing so. It should be made clear at the outset that the latter will not be tolerated. I don't doubt that many arguments can be presented against this position, but the alternative is more and more government and more and more debt.

"They all do it," has been echoed repeatedly by libs justifying Obama's spending. "The Republicans overspent too!" And they are right. The Republicans spent too much. Ronald Reagan spent too much. Bush 41 spent too much and Bush 43 spent way too much. Reagan set fire to the outhouse. Bush 41 burned the tool shed. And Bush 43 let the garage go up in flames. Barack Obama has burned down the local high school and now he's got his eye on town hall.

No individual, business or governmental entity can indefinitely spend more than it takes in. Re-read that last line because it is the simple, self-evident, undeniable truth. Having a printing press and turning out one trillion dollars in monopoly money every year does not change that simple truth.

Anyone still supporting the Obama Regime can only do it by pretending that mathematics simply does not exist.

Nine

SINGLE ISSUE VOTERS

Spare us from the single issue voter! Ed Koch, one time Democratic mayor of New York City, was well known for his town hall meetings. "How am I doing?" he asked the crowd each time. On one occasion he was out in Queens and a member of the audience said the following:

"I voted for you but you disappointed me on your stance on mass transit."

"What's your point?" asked Koch.

"Well, my point is, why should I vote for you the next time?"

"When two guys are running for an office," said Koch, "and you agree with one of them 40% of the time and the other 70% of the time, you vote for the guy you agree with 70% of the time. If you want someone who agrees with you 100% of the time, get your own name on the ballot."

Quite a number of women have told me they won't vote for any Republican because of the "War on Women." So, instead they put a guy back into the oval office because he invites a college girl to speak at the Democratic Convention who wanted free contraceptive devices. The fact that the president had a failed first term, had routinely lied and broken promises is ignored. Many women perceive his action as being sympathetic to women. It never occurs to them they are being manipulated.

Your ears should go up and a little thing ought to run up and down your spine when the government or the media uses military-sounding names for issues: "War on Poverty, War on Drugs, War on Women,

Task Force this or Task Force that, etc." It's a manipulative vote getter and it works only to that extent of getting the votes because that was the only intention. *The only intention.*

A guy had a bumper sticker on his car that read: "I Fish. I Vote." I asked him what he thought of ObamaCare.

"Who cares? I'm going fishing."

Listen to Koch. Try to make some sense out of the whole picture. Don't find one little thing you disagree with and hang your hat on that.

Ten

PRISON REFORM

Prisoners cost about $130 per day or $47,000 per year. That's even more than the tab for sending a kid to college. That is obscene. Some recently built prisons are reminiscent of the palace in the movie *Lost Horizons*. Earlier in this book, drugs are discussed and one of the major benefits of legalizing drugs is that the prison population will be halved and big taxpayer money will be saved. Pass that law and it will be a very long time before another prison is needed.

And when a new one is needed, this is the answer. Remember *The Dirty Dozen?* A group of military prisoners were ordered to build their own shelter. Prisons should be divided into two types regardless of whether it is county, state or federal. One for violent criminals and another for non-violent criminals. The non-violent criminals can be put in army-type barracks. They can maintain vegetable gardens, raise chickens and livestock, do their own cooking and laundry, have libraries, and television sets and maybe just one unarmed guard for every fifty prisoners. Basically, all the guard would have to do is watch the television monitors and do bed check. Their prison unit needs no barbed wire. Its perimeter can be delineated with an 18" white picket fence. Why?

Because if they step over the fence, or hit one of their fellow prisoners with a garden hoe, they immediately go to the violent prison. Do not pass go, do not collect $200, go directly to the big house. The idea of the prison rehabilitating them is nonsense. Don't keep doing something that doesn't work because you would like it to work. I am not talking about torturing prisoners and if every once in a blue moon, one does get rehabilitated on his own, that's fine. Let's just stop pretending that's the goal of the prison. The government exacts revenge for a crime committed with two objectives: the safety of the citizens and to provide a disincentive for others to commit crimes. That's the goal.

When I was a little boy in New Jersey, before the turnpike was built, my family drove down to the Jersey Shore on old Route 1 & 9. As we passed through Rahway, a purple 19th century edifice was visible just 100 yards off the highway. Rahway State Prison, with its turrets and machine gun towers, was the most forbidding place I had ever seen. I knew then as a ten-year old, that I would never do anything in my life that might put me into Rahway State Prison.

I am neither an apologist nor an opponent of Sheriff Joe Arpaio in Arizona. He may well be egocentric. Maybe he even steps over the line from time to time. I don't know. I do know he's right about some things. When prisoners complain about living in a tent without air conditioning, he says "If you don't like it here, don't come back." When he talks about law enforcement overriding his natural human compassion, he's right. I have yet to hear him say anything about Washington that I don't agree with.

Not to suggest or condone other than humane treatment, it is time to reconsider what amounts to luxurious facilities in some prisons. Giving them weight rooms is a form of insanity. I may add that segregating violent and non-violent prisoners is humane in itself. Throwing a white collar criminal into general population? That is inhumane.

The cost of keeping a non-violent prisoner would drop to under $10,000 per annum. The violent prisoner could be given the non-violent status with ten years of non-violent good behavior as an incentive to convicts serving long terms. With fewer prisoners, the cost of maintaining even the violent prisons would drop considerably.

We, as a nation, as a people, have too long thrown money at every problem that came down the pike. It is time to zip up the purse and use common sense instead.

Eleven

PUBLIC SECTOR UNIONS

There was a time, long ago, when two workers could not join together to seek better wages, workplace safety, shorter work hours, or better living conditions. To do so was considered conspiracy and they could be jailed. Many workers were employed in isolated places, most notably, copper and coal miners and railroad construction workers. They were paid not in cash but in company chits which could only be redeemed in company stores and used for rent in company owned houses. Their lives were fully controlled, often by one man.

Men such as Samuel Gompers and attorney Clarence Darrow fought the brave fight to permit collective bargaining. "How can it be illegal to do something with another person that is each person's God-given right to do alone?" asked Darrow.

While there certainly were abuses in the pre-union days, the unions themselves often crossed the line into illegality by participating in government corruption and acts of thuggery, violence and even murder.

But a major misstep was taken by President John F. Kennedy in 1962 when he signed an executive order permitting federal employees to unionize. What followed in the 1960's and 1970's were the creation of unions at all levels of government for police and firefighters, school teachers and other government workers. Today, the largest unions are not in the private but in the public sector.

Public sector unions never made any sense. Not in 1962 and not now. When a union represents policemen or teachers and sits at a table to negotiate for higher wages, the person sitting across the table is not the one who is going to pay the money. He is another government worker. The unions have turned what, fifty years ago, were decent citizens making a contribution into a collection of people, many of whom are whiners.

A public sector worker works for the people. If the workers are underpaid or treated unfairly, their advocate would report ill treatment to the people. The people would decide the issue. If a public sector worker believes he is underpaid, but the people disagree, he is free to choose another line of work. No one is compelled to join the police force, the postal service or to become a teacher.

The teachers union has managed to put something in their contracts that is unreasonable and downright immoral. Tenure. If Satan actually exists, he was involved in the creation of tenure. In essence this is what the teachers' union is saying with tenure:

"After three years, you can't fire a teacher unless he or she is convicted of a crime. Don't ever mention competence or accountability. It is off the table."

There is a basic concept that an employer, private or public, must pay enough that the necessary positions are filled with people who accept these jobs of their own volition, and having accepted the employment, performs to a reasonable standard of competency. One school system of which I am familiar had about 300 teachers and a file with over 700 applications from people who hoped to be hired as teachers.

That situation is indicative that if the the salaries formerly had not advanced beyond perhaps 80% of what currently exists, the school system would still be adequately staffed. The teachers' union opposes those teachers who have demonstrated dedication and excellence being paid more than others. A 3% raise in a given year raises all boats, the slacker with the dedicated.

One can ridicule the army but everybody in the army is seeking the next highest level. Every corporal wants to be a buck sergeant, every captain a major, every brigadier general wants a second star. Everybody gets a proficiency report four times a year and if a soldier does not have an excellent report, he is not going to be promoted.

No such requirement is on the teachers. All they have to do is last three years. Excellence in such a system becomes less and less likely to surface.

About twenty years ago, I was at a school board meeting when a woman gained the floor in the audience participation segment of the meeting. She was a teacher in our school system and had a habit of speaking in a lecturing tone and fixing the person she was addressing with a school-marm disapproving stare. She spoke at virtually every school board meeting about the plight of the teacher. This night she talked about a movie called *Mr. Holland's Opus*. "It's a wonderful movie and there ought to be more like it," she counseled. Following her appeal to the board, as if they produced movies and could follow her advice, I was given the floor.

"There have been more like it. *To Sir With Love, Good Morning Miss Dove, Blackboard Jungle,* and *Goodbye Mr. Chips* come to mind. I am a real estate broker. When Hollywood decides that the real estate broker is the unsung hero, it will be the first time."

At any neighborhood cocktail party, a group will form of three or four guys with the same occupation. They may not even be friends but are sharing job stories. One of the wives will invariably approach the group and say: "No shop talk. Mingle with the others." Now these guys could be postmen, teachers, cops, doctors, lawyers or garbagemen. It doesn't matter. What they were actually saying was the rest of the world doesn't understand or appreciate what they have to do. They are right and they, in turn, don't understand or appreciate people in other walks of life. Live with it. Stop the whining.

How about the cops in New York City? Their final year before retirement is one with an unusually high amount of overtime. Other cops cooperate in letting the would-be retirees pack onovertime that otherwise would have gone to them. Why? Because the pensions are based on the earnings in the last year. A policeman whose base salary is $80,000 and is completing his 20th year of service, works a thousand extra hours at time-and-a-half and pulls in $140,000. His pension is based on 50% of that or $70,000 instead of $40,000. It's criminal.

There are cities going broke because of the demands of the unions and the incompetence and/or dishonesty of those who supposedly negotiated on behalf of the people. They must have thought they'd be lying on a chaise lounge in Boca Raton by the time the fertilizer hit the air conditioner.

Give the public sector employees a strong advocate to speak for them. If they are being treated unfairly, the people being so advised will replace the management of the workers. But get rid of the public sector unions. I don't know what Kennedy could have been thinking. It made no sense in 1962, it makes even less sense today.

Twelve

THE UNITED NATIONS

The United Nations has in sixty-eight years set new standards for impotency. So much so that in the last week (at this writing) with the Russians invading the Crimean Peninsula, the media hasn't even mentioned the U.N. as a possible solution. It was never mentioned because, apparently, the left and the right both know that the U.N. does absolutely nothing. For the last sixty-two years it has been headquartered in a 39 story edifice on the East River in New York City, occupying 18 acres, and serving as a memorial to the words "they meant well."

The U.N. is a failed experiment. That, in itself, is not surprising. I am sure that at the end of World War II many people had little hope for its success but figured it was worth a shot. What is surprising is everyone simply accepting its failure and continuing to support it. By the way, we pay 25% of the tab. Second place pays only 10%

Make it clear to the General Assembly that we are fed up with being taken for granted. We don't mind helping other nations but our first and foremost mission is to benefit the United States of America. We have been far and away the most philanthropic member but we have reached the end of our generosity insofar as the U.N. is concerned. We will continue with that philosophy but are fed up with the pretense of the U.N. We're done.

"Don't let the door hit you on the ass when leaving New York, and don't bother telling us where you're going to set up shop next, because we won't be going there."

Thirteen

COMPROMISE

Compromise. This is a word that has pretty much universal appeal. It is a politically correct word. It's a nice word. Many hold it up as if compromise itself is the objective. Many express opinions that Congress should do more, pass more legislation. I think they should do less. Take two laws that never should have passed off the books for every new law.

I see compromise as a problem. A gin salesman wants to make a dry martini with six parts gin and one part vermouth. The vermouth salesman wants the reverse. So they compromise with three parts each. What do you have? A lousy martini.

Take the young father who runs for the school board at age 28. He has a pure heart and wants to do the right thing as a straight shooter. Five years later he runs for the city council, but the party chairman gets an up front agreement from him to support something he formerly opposed. He compromises. Later he is mayoral candidate but it means more compromising. Then the state assembly and still more compromising and finally in his middle forties, he runs for congress. He is an amiable guy but there is nothing left of the 28 year old. After twenty years of compromising, he now stands for nothing.

Throughout my adult life, some 53 years, I have seen "bipartisan agreement" across the aisle. So much so that the Republican party is now further left of center than the Democratic Party was in 1961. The Democratic party has done little compromising with Republicans but a tremendous amount within their ranks and is today filled with radicals and socialists. Neither party is now worth a tinker's damn. And why?

Because of compromise. With compromise, all you get is watered down decisions. We have compromised ourselves into massive runaway debt. A time will come when compromise is possible. That time is not now. Now we have to get back to being Americans.

Fourteen

LENGTH OF BILLS

The U.S. Constitution has served us well for over two hundred years. It contains less than 9,000 words. The First Amendment contains 45 words, yet it has guaranteed freedom of speech, of the press and of religion for over 220 years.

The Marshall Plan, which rebuilt Europe after World War II, came in at less than 10,000 words. The Affordable Care Act - ObamaCare - is about one million. The average novel is about 300 pages. ObamaCare is about the length of 12 novels! Who actually read it? And if so, who understood it?

I submit that creating such an atrocity was designed to overburden congress and get approval politically. Even Obama doesn't understand it. He's seen fit to change it over thirty times, and to do so without constitutional authority.

Abraham Lincoln once apologized for a particularly long handwritten letter. He said it would be shorter "if I had more time." He meant that it would have been better written and more comprehensible. That bill should have been defeated in both Houses for no other reason than it was one hundred times too long. Even if a congressman agrees with a socialist health care plan, he should have voted against it because it was incompetently written.

Pass a rule in congress. No bill shall exceed 10,000 words. If you can't fit an idea in 10,000 words then make it two bills.

And let's end this crap about earmarks. No unrelated earmarks. If the only way something can become law is to piggyback another bill, then it does not deserve to be a law.

This is just common sense.

Fifteen

THE GOVERNMENT'S APPROACH TO FAILED EXPERIMENTS

A small businessman invests in an ambitious advertising campaign. After a reasonable period he determines that the minimal increase in sales does not justify the additional expense. He aborts the campaign.

A mother buys some pre-packaged vegetables in a tasty sauce in the hope that her children will get their greens in disguised form. But the kids don't like it and won't eat it. She stops buying it.

A lawn-care product promises to get rid of crabgrass. After trying it, the buyer notices the entire lawn has turned brown. He discontinues application of the product.

Decisions to spend money in government are made by other than the owner of the money. Therefore the simple everyday logic cited above does not get introduced. The result is that once created, government programs never go away. Failed experiments just keep right on going like that battery-operated rabbit in TV commercials.

Every project, every department, whether new or old, should be evaluated as to its viability. Is it working? If so, is its objective still needed? If not, get rid of it. Any new program ought to contain a sunset provision: "This program/agency/department shall automatically be concluded in three years unless support can be generated in Congress to reinstate it."

Again, just common sense.

Sixteen

NATIONAL DEFENSE

Why do nightclub owners hire bouncers? The answer is to keep the club free of violence, not to create violence. Even if an unruly customer must be physically removed, he will find himself on the sidewalk with nothing more injured than his dignity, and, if possible, not even that.

To accomplish that end, the ideal bouncer is a large man. Large enough to create a disincentive even among pugnacious inebriates to go the physical route in solving whatever perceived beef they may hold. In short, the bigger the bouncer, the greater the peace and the more gentle manner in which he may conduct himself.

To appease habitual troublemakers, the owner does not replace the big fellow with a semi-big fellow, who, in turn, is replaced with an average sized guy. The smaller the bouncer, the more likely the violence will follow.

We have a problem with some Members of Congress and President Obama who want to downgrade our military to appease potential enemies. These enemies, actual and potential, congratulate themselves for being strong enough to bring about such compromise and become more emboldened to confront and attack us.

We should not give up weapons, take down defensive shields, or for that matter reduce our forces in any manner to pacify some other power. In dealing with other nations, the most important emotion they should feel is fear. They should be afraid to attack us. If in creating the gentle but fearsome giant, we manage to win respect, affection or gratitude for our humanitarian efforts and philanthropic endeavors, that's gravy. But fear is the target.

Nothing in this essay should be interpreted to mean that the military should get a blank check. They are notorious money wasters.

One issue that could gain 100% agreement in both Houses would be to stay out of war if possible. The way, and probably the only way, to accomplish that end is to be strong, very strong.

Seventeen

THE MEDIA AND ITS DERELICTION OF DUTY

Here's a handful -- by no means all -- of Obama gaffes and flubs:

* Referred to 57 states
* Said a whole village was destroyed and 10,000 people died in a Kansas Tornado. It was twelve people.
* "Israel is a strong friend of Israel."
* "We give tribute to our fallen heroes - and I see many of them in our audience today."
* "UPS and FedEx are doing fine. It's the post office that has all the problems," In confusion, he contradicted his own argument why health care is better handled by government.
* His reference to a non-existing Austrian language.
* Referring to a U.S. Navy corpsman (pronounced KOR - MIN) as CORPSE - MIN.
* "...My Muslim Faith..." in a 2008 interview with George Stephanopolis, who tried to bail him out by immediately interjecting "your Christian faith."
* Misspelling of R-E-S-P-E-C-T.
* During 2008 campaign, referred to Joe Biden as "Next President of the United States."

Do these flubs prove that Obama is stupid? Certainly not. They prove that he is human and human beings make mistakes. While these flubs received some media attention, no responsible person ever suggested that they proved Obama was simple minded. But when Gerry Ford or Dan Quayle did it, they were portrayed as buffoons and morons again and again until the majority of Americans truly believed they were *non compos mentis.* In fact, the media has tried to hang the stupid sign on almost every Republican presidential or vice-presidential candidate for the last forty years. Look at the media treatment of Sarah Palin and Michelle Bachmann. Most Americans believe that these women are stupid and hateful. The left wing media was scared to death of both of them. Two beautiful and highly accomplished women who did not blindly kowtow to the liberal line had to be destroyed, and destroy them they did.

Imagine, if you will, a California gold miner who found a handful of nuggets the size of ping-pong balls. Without looking further, he packed up his mules, picks and shovels and headed to a spot on the other side of the mountain.

Picture a league championship baseball team leading by three runs in the seventh game of the World Series walking off the field in the fifth inning giving the game and the series away by forfeit.

These fantasies are tantamount to the behavior of the mainstream media over a host of Obama scandals. What follows is just a handful of Obama scandals -- some sources list over two dozen -- which the media simply stopped investigating and stopped reporting with the idea that if it isn't discussed further, the public will forget about it in a few weeks.

* The IRS targeting Obama's enemies
* Benghazi - Where was Obama that night? The next day he was callously attending a fund raiser. but where was he all night? The mainstream wouldn't even ask. Was Susan Rice acting on her own when she delivered false White House spin on five Sunday News shows? If so, why wasn't she fired? If not, who told her to take that position? Why hasn't the media found out the identity of this person? Did Obama fire anyone for misleading the nation and wrongfully incarcerating the guy who made that video?
* James Rosen, Fox News Reporter: His emails and phone calls and those of his parents were tapped, in a effort to gain some

* dirt which could be used for blackmail. The media talked *ad infinitum* about Nixon's enemies list. Why not Obama's?
* Fast and Furious. A stupid plot instigated by Obama administration that backfired and caused the death of a U.S. Border guard and many, many others. The Obama regime alleges that it was a carry over from Bush 43 and that is a flat out lie.
* General Services Administration $800,000 party in Las Vegas.
* Solyndra: $500 million lost when Solyndra filed for Chapter 11. At the outset, Solyndra's financial position was borderline and hardly a good candidate for government subsidy.
* Black Panthers: The Black Panthers intimidated voters outside a polling place in Pennsylvania were let off the hook by Attorney General Eric Holder. One of those club-bearing men was Samir Shabazz, who has routinely called out for the murder of white people. At a 2009 street festival in Philadelphia, he said: "You want freedom? You're going to have to kill some crackers! You're going to have to kill some of their cracker babies." This is the man that Holder, and therefore, Obama, refused to prosecute. Obama supporters say it was Holder, not Obama. When Holder was not fired, or even denounced, it became Obama, if it wasn't already. Overt anti-white racism committed by the President and the Attorney General. I'm just Joe Schmoe, but that sounds like one hell of a news story to me. How come the mainstream didn't run it?

Do you know who De Marquise Elkins is? How about George Zimmerman?

George Zimmerman made national news for months on end after shooting 17-year old Trayvon Martin during a fight. Zimmerman was armed as a member of a neighborhood watch group. He was acquitted in a controversial trial. I think both of these young men were wrong but I doubt either of them expected to either kill or be killed.

At about the same time, De Marquise Elkins is the black teenager who, during a robbery attempt of a young mother in Brunswick, Georgia, shot her in the leg and then fired a bullet right between the eyes of her 13 month-old baby boy. If you knew who Zimmerman was but did not know who Elkins was, you can thank the liberal mainstream media.

Have you noticed there is a strong media implication that racism is the sole property of white America? Witness the *New York Times* pursuing this fiction by referring to George Zimmerman as a "White Hispanic." That was the first time that term ever rolled past my eardrums. All the news that's fit to print, my ass!

Longtime CBS reporter Sharyl Attkisson resigned from CBS in March of 2014, saying "When I'd begin investigating an Obama scandal, CBS would pull me off."

In 2012 while a half dozen Republicans were jostling for the Presidential nomination, a liberal news magazine ran a photo of Michelle Bachmann, an extremely attractive woman, on its cover. Despite having dozens of photographs to chose from, they picked one which depicted her with a startled expression that made her look unbalanced.

Another liberal magazine ran a cover shortly after the Boston Marathon tragedy showing an air-brushed highly complimentary shot of the surviving bomber. What's wrong with this picture?

Here and there, only in the last year -- not before the 2012 election -- have bits and pieces of criticism of the Obama administration come out in the *New York Times*, *Washington Post*, or MSNBC, but by the next edition they forget about it. They take their mules and go around the mountain.

Obama has often decried any knowledge of something gone bad. He might as well be saying "I didn't know about the IRS targeting the tea party but now that I know I am not going to fire whoever it is that should have told me." He has created a world to live in with deliberate deniability. He empowers lieutenants to do whatever the lieutenant thinks is necessary, with instructions not to report back to the Oval Office. When the manure flies no one is held accountable. No one is fired. If a lieutenant was thrown under the bus and cast out of the Emerald City, the bitter ex-lieutenant might tell the truth. One could only wish Obama would protect our embassy personnel to the same standard.

Going back to 2009, Obama appointed Timothy Geithner Secretary of the Treasury, who was a known tax cheat. Geithner received senate confirmation. A little later, Obama named former Senator Tom Dashiell -- another tax cheat -- as his choice for Secretary of Health and Human Services. When his tax problems were reported, Dashiell withdrew his name. At that time, Barack Obama, in a news conference, accepted blame for making a mistake and said "This one's on me." Lap dog empty suit Brian Williams commented on his broadcast: "Isn't it refreshing to have a President who owns up to a mistake?" No mention was made of the earlier appointment of Geithner. Wasn't that one on Obama as well? Why didn't Williams ask that question? Or any other prominent main stream journalists? Furthermore, within a couple of weeks, Dashiell was appointed as "Health Czar." Apparently slipping Dashiell in the back door without senate confirmation was not considered newsworthy by the main stream either. How about that, Brian Williams? Refreshing, isn't it?

I was on a river cruise down the Danube in the second week of November in 2012, just days after the presidential election. There were only a hundred people on board. Many left the boat on a land tour of Vienna in buses. I was sitting directly behind the tour guide, an Austrian woman. Two Boston women I had met aboard the boat were talking about the election.

"Thank God Romney wasn't elected. How embarrassing would it be to have a President who referred to the Czech Republic as Czechoslovakia?"

"What about," I butted in, "when he referred to Austrians speaking Austrian? Apparently, he didn't know that Austrians speak German and there is no Austrian language. What about that?"

"Oh, I hadn't heard about that. When did Romney say that?"

"He didn't," I answered. "He also didn't say Czechoslovakia. Someone on his staff did and that got morphed into the Romney camp by the left wing media and that got further morphed into Romney. But the Austrian language thing was said by Barack Obama."

"Oh, no," said the woman, "I never heard that."

"I did," said the Austrian tour guide, from the seat in front.

Clearly these Boston ladies get all of their news from liberal sources. But why did the mainstream give Obama a pass on a flub like that?

As further example, I was at a meeting with about a dozen people who were for the most part, liberal. The woman chairing the meeting said she was going to Austria the following week on business.

"I'll have to brush up my German," she said.

"Not according to Obama. He'd have you brushing up your Austrian" I said. "He made reference to the Austrian Language a few months ago."

Several people mumbled words such as "I never heard that."

"It was on Fox News," I answered.

"And you believed it?" said exactly three people in unison.

It is amazing to me that the left has managed to convey to its knee-jerk followers that everything one hears on Fox is false. I have asked many of them who express that sentiment to name a lie that has been spoken on Fox News. I have yet to get an answer to that question. I e-mailed the u-tube of Obama talking about the Austrian language to them. No one acknowledged receiving it.

There are two Cuban-Americans serving in the U.S. Senate. Robert Menendez (D-NJ) and Marco Rubio (R-FL). Both were in the news in February 2013. Allegations were made about Menendez giving favorable treatment in the Senate to a wealthy doctor and clinic owner in Florida. It was further alleged that Menendez accepted free air transportation to the doctor's Caribbean Island House and that he received sexual favors from teen-aged prostitutes.

At the same time, Rubio had been selected to give the counter argument to Barack Obama's State of the Union Address. He had no rostrum but stood in the middle of a TV sound stage. About ten feet away was a low table -- almost an ottoman -- with a bottle of water. Part way through Rubio's answer, he interrupted himself and rather awkwardly stepped across, bent way over to pick up the water and drank a few sips.

Which Cuban-American Senator did the media focus on that week? The conservative Rubio loop was shown over and over and over again. While the Menendez allegations were reported, the coverage appeared to be about one-fifth of Rubio who committed the unforgivable sin of taking a drink of water.

Ten years ago, CBS news anchor Dan Rather set out to sabotage Bush 43's re-election campaign by charging that young Lieutenant Bush had deserted his air national guard unit during the Vietnam War. Rather had acquired a memo that was purported to have been written by the unit's commanding officer supporting this allegation. The commanding officer was no longer living and Rather interviewed his former secretary on camera. He showed her the memo and asked if she remembered the circumstances surrounding the memo. She looked at the memo and said "I didn't type this." Rather asked if there was anyone else in the office who could have typed it. She said "No." Rather then asked her if it was the sort of memo that the colonel would have written about Bush if he had written a memo. The woman refused to offer the opinion that Rather was trying to put into her mouth.

That was over the line even for the mainstream media and Rather got fired. Following that, as some sort of consolation prize for the dour-faced Rather, was a television tribute to him hosted by the late Peter Jennings and Tom Brokaw. Those two men, who up until that time I respected without necessarily agreeing with, spent an hour kissing the smugly superior rump of the otherwise disgraced Dan Rather. Was their journalistic fraternity endorsing the manufacture of news? It appeared so. And what sort of a world did Rather live in that led him to believe that he could do something like that?

Many years ago, Larry King was a guest speaker at the Correspondents Awards Dinner. He said (paraphrased) "You are dedicated journalists, and nothing but your family and country come before that. (pause) Who am I kidding? *Nothing* comes before that! (outburst of laughter from the audience.)"

I believe that is closer to the truth than what we would hope. This fraternity/sorority of journalists routinely behave as if only they count. Notice they never out one of their own. As far as I was concerned, Brokaw and Jennings lost all credibility with the televised canonization of Dan Rather. It would have been more suitable if they court-martialed his superior ass.

I am proud to be an American. I am proud of many things that America has done. I am proud of the Constitution and I am particularly proud of the First Amendment, which, among other things, ensures that the government will do nothing to interfere with freedom of the press. That has worked well for over 220 years. But with that right goes a responsibility. They go together like a horse and carriage, love and marriage. You can't have one without the other. They have a right to freely print and they have a responsibility to tell the truth.

They have not done that. They are not doing that. This is a major problem. In the Forward, I said this is a no-whining zone and that all problems listed would also come with solutions. The leftist mainstream media will remain so for exactly as long as they perceive it to be in their financial interest to do so. In this case, I have no ironclad solution. The only solution I can think of is for each of you to write or call your newspaper, TV or radio station, to say their dereliction of duty has convinced you to no longer read their paper, watch or listen to their news shows. Only when they think it's profitable will they actually report the truth.

Hypocritically, those that control the mainstream media often castigate business people for seeking a profit, while they, themselves, distort the truth and the news to make a profit.

Eighteen

COUNTERFEIT LOGIC AND DON'T LET THE LINGO FOOL YOU

You will notice that many of the talking heads that appear on news shows often carry a designation that appears under their name: "Former Deputy Protocol Director in Clinton Administration" or "Former Chief Campaign Coordinator for Jimmy Carter." Many of the former White House employees or campaign workers are now political pundits on news shows. These people have their own language of political spin.

Some are well-worn trite term such as: ...below the poverty line.... slippery slope....at the end of the day....or zero tolerance. (Shoot the next grade school principal in the ass with a baked apple who suspends a six-year-old boy for pointing a Twinkie and saying "bang-bang.") "Here at Pine Shadow Elementary, we have a zero tolerance for miming weaponry." However, I must admit that "zero tolerance" does accurately describe my feeling for this over-educated, humorless, festering pimple on society's backside. Ask yourself who it is that determines what the poverty line is.

"So at the end of the day, a slippery slope will occur and the American people must maintain a zero tolerance to incorporate inclusion for those below the poverty line...." Disregard everything that person already said and pay no further attention. He or she is a non-thinking puppet.

Criticize the Obama regime for something that went wrong and you will hear someone say "But that was an **unintended consequence**."

That term implies that we, as citizens, can have no expectations that the so-called cream of the Ivy League brain trusts high up in the federal government, will actually think about what the consequences of a given action will be BEFORE THEY DO IT!

This is not the biggest hurdle we face as Americans, but it is the same thinking as other lingo-smiths, who are usually anonymous but should be pointed out. Here is a sample of their handiwork:

"War On Poverty." There is no war on poverty, nor can there be. Poverty is an indistinct subjective term. The politician who declares war on poverty is merely trying to attract the votes of people who think of themselves as poor. Poverty is a carefully chosen word. What does it mean? It used to mean a family that was poor to the extreme. It implied going to bed hungry. Now it's used to describe anyone who makes less than a number that some anonymous bureaucrat in the government sets. I had a childhood friend who lived in a small house with his mother, father, sister, grandfather and uncle. His father was a bus driver and his uncle a policeman. The uncle owned a car -- a pre-war coupe -- but his parents didn't. They had a television set. I don't recall them ever traveling. I thought of them as poor. They thought of themselves as poor. They were certainly thrifty, but they weren't in poverty. Everybody would like to hit the lottery. But there is such a thing as a level of prosperity. Some people's level is relatively low but they are unwilling to do anything to raise it. They would rather exist on what they have than to take a second job or train for a better job or simply to work harder in the job they have. Their first $30,000 in annual income has infinitely greater value than a second $30,000 would have. Leave them alone. Don't brand them as poverty stricken.

For several years I attended a news group in my neighborhood that was at least ninety percent liberal. At one meeting a fellow came up with an idea how unemployed people could be given computer training if they needed it to enable them to earn four or five hundred dollar a weeks at home. I said it was a great idea but because the unemployment insurance benefits had just been risen to 99 weeks, there would be limited incentive to take part. Another man said "anybody who thinks $300 per week will satisfy anyone has not thought it through."

I answered that in many, maybe even most cases, the husband and wife are both collecting and often are working in some underground fashion, including waiting on tables, cleaning houses, or selling goods at flea markets. "The $300 you refer to may well be $1,000. and that could easily reach their level of prosperity." The term "Poverty Line" is more government lingo and manipulation.

"I have been fighting for minimum wage increase in the House." Rank word-smithing. Common political horse manure. He hasn't been *fighting*. Maybe he argued a little, but he wasn't fighting. Not to pile up on the Democratic Party, but they exist only because of a permanent underclass and they do nothing to elevate that group besides saying things like "We're declaring war on poverty!" They know the more prosperous the underclass becomes, the less likely they will vote for the Democratic Party.

Think about these phrases for just a minute when you hear them. Think about what the words actually mean.

A classic attempt to manipulate the public occurred in the week following the passage of ObamaCare. Eight or nine young doctors from a Washington hospital were summoned to the White House for a photo op with the president. Excited about the invite, they showed up properly attired in business suits. Rahm Emanuel took one look at them at said: "No, no, no. You look like stock brokers. Send somebody over to the hospital and get a bunch of those long white coats, with stethoscopes and a couple of those little round mirrors they strap onto their heads." Once fully costumed, then, and only then did a smiling Barack Obama receive the group in the Rose Garden for the photo op with the young medicos appearing to support ObamaCare. The doctors must have felt like idiots. I don't actually know that Rahm Emanuel did that, but somebody did and I can picture him managing the charade. The Dems don't really hold their constituencies in high esteem. What type of mind decided this manipulative fiasco was necessary?

Back to the point, think about this one: The Republicans have declared a War on Women!

Did that happen? What does that mean? Is it the abortion thing? Or does it refer to women generally getting paid less? It can't mean inequality of salary because Barack Obama's female staffers are paid considerably less than his male staffers. It is further obvious that it can't relate to inequality of salary because, as this is being written, it is being reported that the first female executive editor of that paragon of the left, *The New York Times*, has been fired for being pushy. Jill Abramson objected to her male predecessor and even her male deputy assistant being paid more than her. Trouble in paradise? Is the "Gray Lady" a closet male chauvinist pig? My goodness, is the left waging a war on women? Let's declare war on hypocrisy.

Why would Republicans declare war on women? Why would any political party deliberately alienate half the country? Answer: They wouldn't. Logic tells you there is no such thing as a war on women in America and whoever tells you such a thing exists is lying in an attempt to manipulate your vote.

When a political leader uses the phrase "hardworkingamericans" be on guard. That's one word: hardworkingamericans. Manipulation.

Be very wary of politicians or pundits using military terms or metaphors for violence. e.g. "Task Force Milk For Children." Think about that. It implies that one has to get violent to get milk for children to prevent some other group from withholding the milk. Who is that evil group? Why, the Republicans, of course. Just ask Chuck Schumer, Nancy Pelosi or Harry Reid.

A member of the House of Representatives who votes against the milk bill is described as being against children drinking milk. Being opposed to the feds sticking their noses into the milk servings in Iowa grade schools is a statement in favor of the people of Iowa being perfectly capable of taking care of their own children, and not being against children drinking milk. Think about how someone is attempting to manipulate you. Don't fall victim to counterfeit logic.

Harry Reid said Republicans wanted dirty air and water. It sounded like he was describing a Saturday morning cartoon villain, like the evil "Doctor Pollution," who is planning on taking over the world just as soon as it got dirty enough. Harry doesn't have a high opinion of those who vote for him. Then again, maybe he's right. After all, both he and Obama got re-elected talking to their constituencies as if they were in a collective third grade.

Nineteen

THE MINIMUM WAGE

Question: What does McDonald's sell?

Answer: Hamburgers.

Wrong answer. McDonald's sells a replicable system that deals with a major business problem of employees by successfully utilizing the bottom of the work force -- our children!

The stories have gone the route, such as the McDonald's cash registers have pictures of their products on the keys so no math is required of the clerk. I don't know if that is actually true but it's gotten around.

McDonald's has created a system which can employ people who only possess skills that virtually everybody has. When Dr. Christian Barnard performed a successful heart transplant he was the only person in the world that knew how to do it. For a period of time he had no competition, and if he had been so inclined (he wasn't), could demand any fee he chose. The more people that are capable of doing a given job, the less the compensation. I daresay that is true under any form of government. A full-blown Marxist may say that isn't fair, but he might as well say that gravity isn't fair. And how fair is it to pay a person who spent his or her youth studying medicine the same amount as a letter carrier? And what would be the incentive of the would-be doctor?

Minimum wage is a joke; a pathetic effort to win over voters who don't think things through.

If the minimum wage is to be $10 per hour instead of $7.50, does it mean the value of that worker just increased by 33%? If it doesn't mean that, which, of course, it doesn't, then presumably the manager will have to reduce the work force by one in four.

If, on the other hand, he keeps all the kids, then a $3 hamburger just became a $4 hamburger. Of course, then the sales are reduced and someone has to be laid off. All of this is indicative that the government ought to simply butt out!

I haven't heard anyone point out that the minimum wage can also serve as a ceiling wage. With a minimum wage, sameness is introduced. And the sameness will not be an excellent sameness but a mediocre sameness at best. Some kids will work better than others. Left to tend to their own business, management will reward those kids with a higher wage. Under minimum wage restrictions that is less likely to occur. After a while, the good kids say "Why bother going that extra step? We all get paid the same amount anyway."

Under the minimum wage, business is impeded, less kids are working and a disincentive is in place that is counter to good relations between employee and employer.

Liberals argue that currently a full time minimum wage person will earn about $15,000 per annum and that is below some federal poverty line. So what? This is an entry level job and might augment the collective household income above that imaginary line. Almost all such employees are hardly the heads of households. Introducing such a thing as a "poverty line" is more governmental counterfeit logic.

In totality, the minimum wage does not help the kids, the employers, or the customers, but it does help elect phony politicians who claim to be speaking for the poor, but are not actually doing so.

Of course, the implied premise in this movement is that private business is corrupt and evil and will take advantage of poor people. When you work under a false premise, the conclusion must be false. If you elect pi to be 4.13 instead of 3.14, you can do everything else right, but the rocket you're building ain't going to land on the moon.

Minimum wage is the product of a false premise. Call your congressperson and object to it.

Twenty

RED STATES/ BLUE STATES

What started as nothing more than a color-coded visual on TV election night news shows, has developed into something of a division akin to the relationship of the 1860 states. It is deplorable.

The most arrogant piece of trash I ever saw went around the INTERNET in 2008. It talked about the blue states had most of the colleges, theaters, intellectuals, hospitals. etc. And if the red states wanted to get into wars, then they and they alone should provide the soldiers.

I am recalling it totally from memory. It went on at some length implying only ignorance could explain being a red state. At the time, it occurred to me they omitted that the blue states also had most of the crime, the highest taxes and the most debt. They also forgot that the worst run cities in America were Democratically controlled and had been so, in most cases, for fifty or more years. And those cities are found where? The blue states. Another thing that escaped their attention was what Woodrow Wilson, Franklin Roosevelt, Harry Truman and Lyndon Johnson had in common beside membership in the Democratic Party.

Had they considered it, they might have noticed that World War I, World War II, Korea and Viet Nam all began during Democratic Administrations. And when they toss around innuendo about racism in the red states, they ought to be reminded that the Democratic Party ran KKK member John Sparkman for vice-president of the United States in 1952. Adlai Stevenson, a decent guy, was spared the humiliation of being photographed with Sparkman in raised victorious hand-in-hands. If someone feels that's ancient history, consider that only a few years ago, Bill Clinton lauded Senator Robert Byrd of West Virginia. Senator Byrd had, much earlier in his career, also been a member of the KKK. Old Slick Willy pooh-paahed that saying "He just did that to get elected."

What are we supposed to think about that? Oh, he just did it to get elected? Well, I guess it's all right then. What can that mean but that Bill Clinton holds the view that anything a pol says to get elected is okay?

But some years earlier, when Trent Lott, then Republican Senate Majority Leader, did virtually the same thing by heaping praise on retiring Senator Strom Thurmond, he was crucified by the mainstream media.

We are one country with fifty states. This color line designation is divisive. Let's get rid of it. Write or call your newspaper, TV and radio stations and tell them to refrain from using it.

Twenty-One

HOLLYWOOD LIBERALS

75 years ago, Hollywood couldn't wait for the U.S. to declare war. They anticipated big money to be made from war films and they were right. They produced propaganda films in the late 1930's and very early 1940's: *The Dawn Patrol* (1938), *The Fighting 69th* (1940) and *Sergeant York* (1941), to name a few, before America entered the war. Then the Niagara of war films were made, and they didn't stop when the war was over. World War II was, and to some extent is to this day, a cash cow. Hollywood is the show business capital of the world -- with emphasis on the word business. It was good business for Hollywood to be pro-war.

The actors and actresses that we thought of as being larger than life were mere employees and usually did as they were told. They made appearances on behalf of servicemen and movies about USO canteens. Greer Garson poured a soldier a cup of coffee and Jimmy Durante gave him a doughnut. Some of the actors were drafted and others actually enlisted. With very little exception, the visible Hollywood people presented a pro-war posture. When the Korean War came along, the public was not eager to experience wartime austerity again, and were not enthusiastic. Neither was Hollywood. Vietnam was downright unpopular, youth was rebelling and protesting, and Hollywood made almost no movies about it. Show Biz is a business.

In 1992 a Long Island teen-ager named Amy Fisher shot the wife of her boyfriend, Joey Buttafuoco. It probably was the media event of the year. Hollywood jumped on it and almost simultaneously put out three TV movies with three different casts. In all three movies, the character of the victim, Mary Jo Buttafuoco, was almost non-existent. One of the movies was sympathetic to Amy Fisher, one to Joey Buttafuoco, and one to both of them. All three obscured the truth. In watching Alyssa Milano's portrayal, the viewer could relate to the sweet face of Alyssa and hope she wouldn't be too severely punished for shooting a woman in the face at point blank range.

It brings to mind those African nature films about wild animals. One show's focus is on a coalition of cheetahs, and you're rooting for the hungry mother cheetah to run down an impala so she can feed her cubs. The next month, the show is on impalas and the viewer is praying the impala can escape the big bad cheetah.

Hollywood is incredibly adept at manipulation. And when they want to sell a message, the truth is not on their agenda.

The actors themselves are by and large self-centered. Most are extremely aware of the fragility of their careers. While being relatively intelligent, they are often immature, paranoid and totally apathetic about things political but they've been told what sells. What sells is liberalism.

Six or seven years ago on one of the talk shows, I watched a little fellow who acted on a second rate sitcom in a supporting role. I don't think I ever knew his name but recognized him only because he is very odd looking. He surely knew he'd only have a couple of minutes on camera. His agent probably coached him with a list of items he must talk about. Something like this: 1) Mention his TV show 3 or 4 times. 2) Relate an anecdote about his relationship with a well-known actor. 3) Bad-mouth George W. Bush by referring to him as being stupid.

So this little gnome mechanically followed his agent's advice, and remembered about the Bush thing only as the off-stage producer is waving him off the couch. As he stood up, he gratuitously injected a nasty comment about the president. What stood out was his transparency. Other show biz people are better at it, but they routinely do it.

Mostly beginning with college, many have been told over and over again that liberalism is superior to conservatism. It is hammered home repeatedly that liberals are more intelligent and more caring than conservatives. Many highly intelligent people actually believe that. They are so indoctrinated, brainwashed, that they simply never turn their analytical skills to that issue.

Twenty-five years ago, my son was selected to attend "Governor's School of Public Affairs" in our state of residence. 100 of the state's top students were chosen between junior and senior year in high school. The kids boarded at a local college for the month of July. My son possessed largely conservative views. He was more interested in politics, even as a child of ten or eleven, than in games involving balls.

The school boasted faculties of highly qualified college professors from some of the most acclaimed institutions of higher learning in the nation. My son spent most of his time as a foil, arguing against a wall of left wing views, but he made many friends and still goes to reunions of this group every few years.

At the conclusion, the school invited the parents to an afternoon tea to meet the visiting faculty. One such professor was a Catholic nun in full habit, who held a doctorate and full professorship at Harvard. This is what she said to us:

"Your son is a fine and caring young man. When I got to know him I realized his actual character belies his political opinions."

I answered: "While it may be politically expedient to put forward views that Volkswagen drivers are better human beings than Cadillac drivers, I am disappointed that someone of your academic standing would hold such a sophomoric opinion. It doesn't speak well of you or Harvard."

Despite her education, it never occurred to the nun that the parents of a very decent young man could be anything but liberal themselves. Whatever her shortcomings, she certainly wasn't trying to be offensive. The false premise was so deeply embedded in her thinking, she never questioned it. Although being a highly intelligent woman, she never analyzed the concept that conservatives were evil.

If, by way of experiment, every day some television talk show discussed a homosexual affair between Joseph Stalin and Adolf Hitler, in a matter of a few weeks it would be accepted by millions. No amount of fact presentation to the contrary would ever totally eradicate the falsity. Such is the way with liberalism. Oft-repeated lies have a way of being accepted as fact.

Tom Hanks, clearly an intelligent man, was once asked a political question. I don't recall what it was. I'm almost certain that Hanks doesn't have political thoughts, and has routinely and wisely chosen to keep out of public political conversations. This time, however, he was caught off guard and gave a rather shallow brief answer. A day or two later, on camera, another interviewer asked him to expand on his answer. His face went blank and he turned and walked off camera without a word.

Those actors who do hold conservative views tend to keep quiet until such time as they become so successful or so old that they can get away with it. In any case, the statements of actors, liberal or conservative, carry much more weight than their worth. Often, the actor (or actress) is nothing more than an egocentric emotional child.

In summation and in general, entertainers should be ignored when they talk politics. They have a right to speak and you have a right not to pay attention.

Apply the same skepticism to movies and TV shows as you do to the commercials and for the same reason. Your life's experience has taught you that eating in Subway restaurants is not going to improve your sex life. Both the show and the commercial are trying to sell you something. Selling is manipulating. Use your common sense. Don't allow yourself to be manipulated.

Hollywood doesn't make opinion. They are not that courageous. They wait until the wind blows and then jump on the bandwagon. Show biz is a biz.

Twenty-Two

MIDDLE CLASS LIBERALS

A very interesting thing happened on February 18, 2014. An article appeared in the *Harvard Crimson* written by a 21 year-old student editor named Sandra Korn. Sandra wrote "Let's give up on academic freedom in favor of justice." She goes on to insist that Harvard stops guaranteeing students and professors the right to hold controversial views and conducting research putting liberalism in a negative light. Sandra is overly impressed with her own intellectuality but does not recognize her own immaturity. Getting rid of conservative professors at Harvard could probably be handled in a Cooper Mini, but it is not Sandra's opinions that are interesting.

It was the non-reaction of the liberal media. Not a word. You could hear the crickets chirping. I envision a conversation between a power broker of the progressive movement whose name would not be familiar to the man on the street. He is a behind-the-scenes guy and knows how to extort money from corporations to fund liberal ideology.

"Sandra. You can't actually *say* you want to do away with free speech."

"But why not? Don't we want to silence the right wing?"

"Of course! But you can't do it that way. We'll do it by end-runs. Suspending their FCC licenses, buying up their newspapers or by ridiculing them. There's no defense against ridicule. Listen, half of our supporters are people who are basically apolitical. They're not really interested in politics. But we have been indoctrinating them for decades. Most of them grew up in comfortable surroundings and we have succeeded in making them feel guilty for having two televisions and central air. Like you. You lived in a million dollar house in Basking Ridge, New Jersey.

"We managed to brain-wash them that liberalism is for the intelligent and the caring while conservatives are evil, greedy white men who are racist and homophobic."

"But conservatives are greedy, evil, white people, aren't they?"

"Of course they are, Honey, but you get that across very subtlety. Most of our followers are everyday decent people. We've convinced them they have to be liberal if they are to be thought of as intelligent and caring. Since they don't really study politics anyway, they took a short cut and identified themselves as liberals. They vote liberal. When a conservative wants to argue with them, they really don't know what to say so they attack the conservative to end the conversation. They accuse him of being angry or racist or uncaring. All they want is to end the conversation They often say that you shouldn't discuss politics or religion."

"So what's the problem?"

"The problem is that if you openly say you want to silence the opposition, you will lose them. They're apathetic, but they're Americans. If you say no more free speech, they would stop being apathetic and would rise up in alarm. We could lose half of them. We have the power now. That's what our movement has been all about for decades. But power is a fragile thing. We're strong, but not strong enough to curtail free speech. We could lose our followers if they thought it was about power and not about altruism.

"A reformed alcoholic once told me that it was easier to give up alcohol than it was to give up his friends. That's how it is with our followers. They have too much invested in appearing liberal to change so long but you can't rock the boat by ending free speech.

"Their jobs, their friends, their relatives, their religion are often contingent upon being liberal. And they don't have to know anything about politics. All they have to do is nod in agreement with other liberals and badmouth a conservative now and then. Hell, we don't want them to know anything. But tell them no more free speech for the right wing and it will occur to them that if the right wing can be silenced in Harvard then the left wing can be silenced at Notre Dame. They're apathetic but not stupid.

"After all, Sandra, these people are Americans, and deep down, love America."

***

The above conversation is from my imagination but I daresay it occurred. If it only existed in my mind, and didn't actually occur, why didn't the mainstream media report on Sandra Korn's fascist views? Who is it in the *New York Times*, CBS, NBC, ABC, CNN, or MSNBC that gave the order to ignore the story of an editor of the *Harvard Crimson* wanting to throw the First Amendment in the toilet? These entities live on the First Amendment. And yet, they kept silent. Could it be they were hoping a Republican would say that?

The self-congratulated intelligentsia of the media might, at some point, wake up and recognize that with unchecked power, the progressives could march backward with flying banners and brass bands to the Third Reich and the Spanish Inquisition. But the media intelligentsia hasn't gotten there yet.

Is that overstated? I don't think so. Remember the Group of 88 at a major east coast university? In 2006 a black woman falsely accused three white lacrosse players of raping her. One month later, 88 professors signed an advertisement virtually convicting the boys. No presumed innocence, no due process. It was as if they had said "We don't need to presume innocence - we're liberal professors." The irony of this is that even if the boys had been guilty, they would still have been wrong. All that higher education and no one stopped and asked "What are we doing?"

The university in question settled lawsuits with the boys for undisclosed amounts. Many of those professors went on to higher paying jobs in the same school or other universities, including Cornell, Vanderbilt, Harvard and the University of Chicago. Those 88 professors, who were supposedly there for the benefit of the students, made a decision to ruin the lives of three of their charges. They should have gone to prison for conspiracy to deny due process of the law. Instead they were protected by their university.

The school was concerned only about damage control and spent an undisclosed amount in legal fees to protect the school and the Group of 88 as well as major settlements to each of the three boys. If I had to guess how much of endowment money they spent, I would place it at $35 million. If I was an alum of that place, not only would I never contribute another cent, but I would sue for the return of earlier donations. I would also take a razor blade to the rear window of my car to remove any of the school's decals.

The over-zealous Sandra Korn ignores the constitution and looks down her nose at merchants, policemen and everyday people. An internship at the Holocaust Museum might do her some good. But while deifying Che' Guevara and the Black Panthers, she spilled the beans as to what the unseen leaders of the progressive movement really want. And they respond by saying nothing. Absolutely nothing.

Twenty-Three

POLITICAL CORRECTNESS AND TAKING/ GIVING OFFENSE

St. Patrick's Day, New York City, 1967 -- A group of about a dozen young men gathered at the curb of 5th Avenue in anticipation of the parade. They had a blue-collar look to them; sandy and auburn hair and blue eyes were in evidence. One had curly, very dark hair and that push-nose look common among the black Irish. They had already begun celebrating. Kelly, Mulrooney, Gallagher and O'Donohue to call them something. They had hand-written placards that read *MISTER LINDSEY, WHY DON'T YOU LIKE THE IRISH?* Another said *NO LINDSEY GO BRAGH.* And several others of the like. Their manner was jocular in anticipation of holding up the placards for Mayor John Lindsey to see when he passed their spot while leading the parade. They were having fun. If I knew whatever Lindsey's slight on the Irish was, I have forgotten. It couldn't have been much. Whatever it was, they, as Irish-Americans, took offense and were enjoying it immensely. That was the first time that I realized that people as individuals or as part of a group take pleasure in being offended by some authority leader or entity. I have noticed it hundreds of time since. I know guys who will tell the same story over and over again of something offensive their boss said forty years ago. They like telling the story. It is pleasurable to recall the offense.

The ultra-sensitive left has decided that no one can ever be offended at any time. Therefore there can be no Christmas decorations at schools because there may be a non-Christian child who will take offense. The Star Spangled Banner can't be sung and the Pledge of Allegiance can't be recited for fear that someone, somewhere, will be offended. This thinking is a first cousin to the idea that every kid gets a trophy in little league.

The irony of this is that over 80% of America is Christian and they take offense that their kids don't get to sing Christmas carols at school.

This political correctness -- and its self-appointed police -- is not about what has been spoon fed to the liberal class. If it just got rid of some nasty words, I would have no problem with it. But that's not what it's about. It's about thought control and punishment -- *and it's about power!* Knee jerk thought control. A couple of years ago, my daughter attended her children's grammar school function and in conversation, she referred to Nelson Mandela as a black man. One of the local PC police-persons jumped on that: "We don't say black anymore. We say African-American," (in a condescending tone). My daughter replied "I didn't know he had become naturalized."

Have you ever asked yourself who is the man (or woman) behind the curtain and makes the decisions as to what is or is not politically correct? Who is the PC Wizard?

Whoever it is, he or she has immense power. Let someone make a ethnic comment or some negative reference to homosexuals and his career is wiped out. There are people who get less punishment for armed robbery.

The "PC Criminal of the Month" last month was Brendan Eich, who was forced to step down as CEO of Mozilla Corporation. Eich is a brilliant computer tech guy, who in 2008 donated $1,000 to oppose same-sex marriage. He donated his money. It wasn't reported that he said anything. When that fertilizer hit the air conditioner early in 2014, he was compelled to step down.

Past "PC Criminals of the Month" go back to Earl Butz, Nick the Greek, Paula Deen and the "PC Criminal of the Decade" Don

Imus. Imus, who mimicked street rappers in calling the Rutgers girls basketball team "a bunch of nappy-headed ho's" was figuratively forced to his knees in apology and exiled from television for a couple of years. Once again, a double standard was in place. Nobody said boo about the rappers. The rappers, being black, were judged by some lesser standard because the PC police consider them to be lesser. Nothing could be a more obvious racist view and yet it is never, *never* mentioned.

Incidentally, the girls basketball team enjoyed the controversy immensely. They were delighted to pout before the television cameras. They'll go through life talking about it.

Getting back to Brendan Eich and same-sex marriage. I personally have no opposition to same-sex marriages. I balk at pundits suggesting that it's perfectly normal, but if the gays want to get married to one another, let them. "Normalcy" is not mandatory in America. But I totally oppose that Lesbian, Gay, Bi-sexual, Trans gender (LGBT) group. It's as if they're saying: "Somebody disagrees with us, we take him out." The fair-minded gays should speak out against that group. It is also interesting that the LGBT is not backing one of their own running for congress in California, Carl DeMaio. Why not? He's a Republican. They're following the leads of women's group and the NAACP in saying "We'll only support you if you're a liberal Democrat."

Consider this firestorm of strong-arming the Washington Redskins to change their name. The PC police claim it is a slur on native Americans. Hogwash! It's a tribute. It signifies courage and fighting spirit. The same is true for the Cleveland Indians, the Atlanta Braves, and the Kansas City Chiefs. About twenty years ago, while Jane Fonda was married to the owner of the Atlanta Braves, Ted Turner, an activist group tried to make the Atlanta fans stop making tomahawk chops with their hands.

Take note that todays activists are discussing only the Redskins. If they can win that one, they'll go after the other three, plus hundreds of minor league or college teams. One knee-jerk buffoon said to me: "If even one person is offended, it shouldn't be done." I told her she should shut up because she was offending me. I watched one guy on television, who claimed to be a native American, but looked like a Presbyterian minister, object to the Redskins and called it a slur. Hollywood would have cast this guy as an Indian only to play opposite to Elizabeth Warren in the role of Pocahontas. I could see none of the physical characteristics of a native American about him, but I could see that he was enjoying taking offense so much he probably couldn't see straight.

The next thing one might expect is Obama Regulatory Czar Cass Sunstein, who championed an idea that animals should be able to sue humans, will be attacking the Chicago Bears or the Detroit Tigers for the unauthorized use of bear and tiger likenesses.

This entire political correctness movement has become a parallel third world judicial system. Witch hunt is an overused analogy but I can't think of a better fit. Judgment is passed without trial or appeal. Cross a line that is anonymously drawn and the punishment is unbelievably harsh.

Every decent American, left or right, should resist this faceless, nameless, alternative authority. It is a malignant growth in a place where academic freedom and free speech are held dear.

Twenty-Four

PHOTO I.D. TO VOTE?

On every news show there will be at least one poll. The question can be on any topic: ObamaCare, raising the American flag at schools, foreign policy, etc. The interesting thing is the total never adds up to 100%. It might say: Approve 56% Disapprove 33%. That's only 89%.

I would like to see a third category labeled: No Flipping Idea Because I Don't Read Newspapers And Every Time The News Comes On TV I Switch to Gilligan's Island Reruns.

I am not questioning these people's right to vote but what is the point of them doing so? If they vote, it really gives two votes to whoever it was that drove them to the polling place.

Casting a ballot is a sacred responsibility and we now have the technical ability to require anyone voting to properly identify him or herself. This notion that it creates a hardship on some people is nonsense. Driver's licenses, passports, and county I.D. cards all have photographs. Veterans Affairs cards have a photo.

Voter fraud does exist. In 2008, 57 voting districts in Philadelphia recorded 100% of the votes were cast for Obama. In 2012, 59 voting districts in Philadelphia went 100% for Obama. (Checked out in Snopes). 100%! In those thousands of people, even if we accept that every last one wanted Obama, are we expected to believe that not even one of them pulled the wrong lever by mistake? There's an old story about when Lyndon Johnson first ran for congress, several hundred people voted in alphabetical order. Mayor Jimmie Walker openly joked about Tammany Hall shenanigans in stuffing ballot boxes.

I strongly suggest that the same people who have no opinions on any topic presented to them are the ones who can't seem to be able to get a photo I.D. card.

Several years ago, a young couple exposed A.C.O.R.N., a so-called community organizing group. James O'Keefe and Hannah Giles should have received the Pulitzer Prize. Aside from other nefarious activities A.C.O.R.N. was active in registering previously unregistered voters. An investigation showed their field people were not overly respectful of the ballot box. Many irregularities were discovered including one registrant by the name of Mickey Mouse. Why should a responsible adult need the help of a community organizer to vote? And if they only register because of some external push, they are extremely likely to be in that 10 or 12% who basically have no opinion. If someone is a shut-in, that's one thing. If not and they want to vote in their country's elections, they should get their own fanny down to the county hall and register and then get that same fanny to the polling place with a picture I.D. If they can't manage that, then voting wasn't very high on their agenda in the first place and it would have been if they had any idea what was going on. This idea that we must have more input from the most ignorant people in the nation is something that no intelligent person would support without an ulterior motive. When you hear a pol express opposition for photo I.D.'s, ask yourself what is the motive. There can be only one motive. He wants people to vote illegally.

In the movie *A League of Their Own* about a professional women's baseball league during World War II, there is a scene in which the star player, played by Geena Davis, is quitting the team in mid-season. The manager (Tom Hanks) is trying to dissuade her. She says "It just got too hard."

He says "It's supposed to be hard. Otherwise everybody would do it."

That's how voting should be. This movement to make it easier and more convenient to vote cheapens and undermines the process. Furthermore, where is the dignity of those Americans who don't object to being patronized?

In 2008, comedian Al Franken ran for the U.S. Senate seat from Minnesota against Republican Norm Coleman. The election was tight but after the polls closed Coleman was ahead by several hundred votes. A recount was ordered and when it was over, Coleman's original total had hardly moved and Franken's increased by over 500, and he was declared the winner.

Interfering with the election process should draw a longer prison sentence. Anyone conspiring to fraudulently alter the outcome of an election should get to spend the next ten general elections in the slammer.

Recently, there was a street interviewer who asked people how they felt about the recent death of Franklin Delano Roosevelt at a very advanced age. About a half-dozen individuals or couples were shown, none of whom knew that FDR had been dead for 69 years. One couple was a pleasant looking pair in their sixties. They very nicely replied their prayers were with his family and it was a sad day to lose this very great man. Of course, the interviews shown were limited to the ones that didn't know that FDR was dead. But it was still shocking that many people walking around could be so ignorant. What's even more shocking is that they signed releases to allow the interviews to be aired.

The Democratic party has strongly opposed required photo I.D.'s for voting but also opposed late arriving absentee ballots from American military personnel -- through no fault of their own -- serving abroad. Could the reason be that they expect the ignorant to vote Democratic but they expect the G.I.'s to vote Republican?

Legitimate absentee ballots are one thing, but this early voting is counter-productive. Next they'll be saying you can vote on line. That just opens the door to more fraud. Some things shouldn't be made easier.

There was a well-written, well-acted, left-leaning television show called *West Wing*. On one episode, Martin Sheen, playing the President, came down with the flu and was confined to robe and slippers in his apartment. A Presidential aide came up to gain his signature on some document. Having gotten it, the staffer began to leave the room and the President stopped him.

"Yes, Mr. President?"

"I've been watching television."

"Yes, sir?"

"This show had three young women as guests. All three claimed their husbands were cheating on them with their mothers. You understand, these young men were having sex with their respective mothers-in-law?"

"Yes, sir?"

"Then they brought the husbands out and everybody began shouting. They sent a couple of big guys up on the stage to keep the peace. But then they brought out the three mothers and all hell broke loose. Fist-fighting mothers and daughters and furniture being thrown about."

"Yes, sir, Mr. President. What about it?"

"Well, my question is, do you think these people vote?"

Just two days before I am writing this, Rush Limbaugh was named as Children's Book Author of the Year, by The Children's Book Council. The Huff Post Media, unhappy with this event, interviewed someone involved who criticized the voting process, supposedly done by children. Apparently there are several ways a child can vote and one of them is on line. It was mentioned that an adult could do the voting on line multiple times, implying that Limbaugh's award was questionable.

How does it come to pass that the Huff Post Media, who is wildly opposed to showing I.D.'s to vote, expresses deep concern with the integrity of children's ballots in an organization nobody ever heard of?

Demand of your congressperson that he or she support required voter photo I.D.'s. Make it clear to him or her that failure to do so is supporting voter fraud. Keep the ballot box sacrosanct.

Twenty-Five

TAKING THE FIFTH

This is the shortest essay in the book. Any American has the right to go into court or before congress and remain silent. Everyone has the right to refuse to answer questions under the provisions of the fifth amendment to the United Sates Constitution. It's a right. And that includes federal employees such as Lois Lerner.

Ms. Lerner, however, enjoys no such right to her employment, her health plan or her pension. The moment when she took the fifth in answer to questions being put to her by a congressional inquiry, she spit in the face of those people who have employed her -- all of us -- and she should have been immediately fired with total loss of all benefits.

Let the word go out to other federal employees that you don't take the fifth when being questioned about your federal job without losing it.

Twenty-Six

THE BIGGEST PROBLEM OF THEM ALL: US

When Joe Biden got caught in numerous acts of plagiarism back in 1987, I recall conversations that from now on, politicians are going to have to be more careful with what they say, what with Lexis-Nexis and the advent of the INTERNET - because one's words become permanently etched and easily retrieved.

But we never anticipated the time would come when a progressive mass media and a citizenry would simply give a pass to someone sitting in the Oval Office. These acts of ignoring the president's words and promises have conditioned him to say whatever he wants with the full expectation that he will not have to explain himself, nor even apologize. One example follows of Barack Obama on the campaign trail in Fargo, North Dakota on July 3, 2008:

> "The problem is -- is that the way Bush has done it over the last eight years, is to take out a credit card from the Bank of China in the name of our children driving up national debt from five trillion dollars from the first forty-two Presidents. Number forty-three added four trillion dollars by his lonesome so that we now have over nine trillion dollars of debt that we are going to have to pay back. $30,000 for every man, woman and child. That's irresponsible -- It's unpatriotic."

After only five and one-half years, under the Obama administration it is now over $55,000 per citizen, with no end in sight. It is as if the country has simply accepted that our nation can continue to spend ten dollars for every six we take in. And that, not Barack Obama, is the problem.

After all, President Obama will be finished in two plus years -- unless he figures out a way to do a third term -- but we will still have the liberal mass media who gave him license to behave in such fashion. And we will still have the citizenry who permitted the whole thing through complacency, apathy, and blind knee-jerk naiveté.

In the late 1960's and early 1970's, the liberal media was all over Vice-president Spiro Agnew. As usual, they tried to make a Republican look stupid. I worked in New York City and found myself in a sea of liberals. I defended Agnew routinely.

When it turned out that he was a tax cheat and had taken payoffs while Governor of Maryland, I was furious. If I had found myself alone with him in an elevator, I would have punched him in the nose. I initiated conversations about Agnew, admitting I had been wrong, very wrong. But I haven't been disappointed with a politician since then, because disappointment only comes with surprise.

Ask yourself why some reporter never approached Obama and said:

> "Mr. President, in your Fargo, North Dakota speech the day before Independence Day in 2008, you chastised Bush 43 for running up four trillion in debt in eight years. Irresponsible and unpatriotic, you said. But you've managed to run up debt by seven-point-five trillion in only two-thirds of that time. Now, it would be rude to ask you if that means that you have been more than twice as irresponsible and more than twice as unpatriotic as President Bush, but don't you think that at least you owe President Bush a sincere public apology?"

Fat chance! Remember Arthur Fonzarelli? "Fonzie" on *Happy Days?* Fonzie was not good at apologizing. The words just wouldn't come. "I'm sor-sor-sor. I was wr-wr-wr."

Well, there are at least two people in the world less likely to accept blame and admit their screw-ups than Fonzie. One is Al Sharpton, of Tawana Brawley-Wappingers Falls, New York fame and the castigation of the three Duke Lacrosse players, just to name two things that he has never apologized for. The second one is Barack Obama.

But again, it is not Barack Obama that is the problem. It is us. We are the ones that looked the other way. We are the ones who tolerate, if we even know, of the downplay of certain news stories that are important and the highlighting of others that are not important. We permit mass media to treat us as if we had the attention span of a sponge. We are the ones that will still be here when Barack Obama is off making a huge living as a guest lecturer and author of his memoirs. And if we let it happen once, it can happen again, and that is our biggest problem. Us.

I'm not talking about ignorant people. I'm talking about educated people. I was at a small gathering at Christmas last winter and a political discussion ensued. An educated man, a certified public accountant, actually, said, in summation, "But you'll have to admit that the most intelligent people hold liberal, not conservative, views." How a man who has made a career of balancing budgets can support Barack Obama with a fiscal policy of endlessly spending $10 for every $6 in income, and consider himself intelligent for doing so is a mystery right up there with those big stone heads on Easter Island. His voting, his opinions, are purely emotional, but because of his higher education, he assumes them to be based on intellect.

"You may not agree with his politics but you'll have to admit that Obama is very intelligent." If I've heard that once, I've heard it a dozen times. I don't have to admit it. Maybe he is and maybe he isn't. But if he is, then there's a built-in condition that goes with that; what appears to be the most inept presidency in my lifetime is actually a deliberate attempt to bring America down. The incompetency of the Obama administration is either real or contrived. Either way, he was a poor choice.

A guy I know with a doctorate said "I like the way he {Obama} dances down the steps of Air Force One. He's got that loose-jointed Fred Astaire thing going." Fortunately I wasn't armed at the time. All those years in school would have been equally well spent in a coma.

Still another real smart guy, Pat Conroy, the author, displayed the arrogance of the left very well. In his novel *Beach Music*, his hero and main character is named Jack McCall. McCall helped out his friend's father, a politically conservative marine general stranded in Rome, with a cash loan. McCall (and therefore Conroy) refers to the act as demonstrating the "natural superiority of the liberal." I think Conroy is still rebelling against the Great Santini. If that isn't arrogance, then Alec Baldwin is a modest and unassuming guy.

Here's the big rub. Where the hell are the platoons, the battalions, hell, the whole armies of people that supported Obama coming forth to say "I made a mistake." I am not seeing anyone in private life admitting it. I have seen damn few in public life. Donald Trump, for one, but he doesn't count because he pretends not to have supported Obama in the first place, which he did.

The only one that comes to mind is Barbara Walters. I am not a fan of *The View* but I watched it one day back in 2008 because I knew John McCain was the guest. Barbara was terrible. She treated McCain disrespectfully and with something akin to anger that he would dare to oppose Barack Obama.

But I had to give her credit last winter. She appeared on Piers Morgan's show on December 18th, 2013. Barbara Wawa said this in response to the declining popularity of Obama:

> "He made so many promises, we thought he was going to be -- I shouldn't say this at Christmastime, but -- the next messiah.
>
> "And the whole ObamaCare, or whatever you want to call it, that affordable health act. It just isn't working for him, and he's stumbling around on it. And people feel very disappointed because they expected more."

The next messiah. Walters at least admitted it. After listening to an Obama speech, Chris Matthews said he felt "this thrill going up my leg," *New York Times* columnist David Brooks said "I was sitting on his [Obama's] couch and looking at the crease in his pant and I thought.......

he's going to be a very good president." Are these people certifiable? But what about all of you? Is this how to pick a candidate for President of the United States?

There are many who fear that we have passed the point of no return. Passed the tipping point, so to speak, and America's days are numbered. They may be right. But hope springs eternal. Another liberal administration will surely do us in, but I hope we have learned our lesson. However, the lack of people coming forth and saying so is alarming. If America elects another lightweight because we think he or she is the messiah, or dresses well, or is cool, then we deserve to lose our country.

It won't be the first time it happened.

www.ingramcontent.com/pod-product-compliance
Lightning Source LLC
Chambersburg PA
CBHW022117170526
45157CB00004B/1678